Paul Schrader |

Contemporary Film Directors

Edited by James Naremore

The Contemporary Film Directors series provides concise, well-written introductions to directors from around the world and from every level of the film industry. Its chief aims are to broaden our awareness of important artists, to give serious critical attention to their work, and to illustrate the variety and vitality of contemporary cinema. Contributors to the series include an array of internationally respected critics and academics. Each volume contains an incisive critical commentary, an informative interview with the director, and a detailed filmography.

A list of books in the series appears
at the end of this book.

Paul Schrader |

George Kouvaros

**UNIVERSITY
OF
ILLINOIS
PRESS**
URBANA
AND
CHICAGO

Frontispiece courtesy Paul Schrader Productions.

© 2008 by George Kouvaros
All rights reserved
Manufactured in the United States of America
1 2 3 4 5 C P 5 4 3 2 1
∞ This book is printed on acid-free paper.

Library of Congress Cataloging-in-Publication Data
Kouvaros, George.
Paul Schrader / George Kouvaros.
p.   cm. — (Contemporary film directors)
Includes bibliographical references and index.
ISBN-13 978-0-252-03306-3 (cloth : alk. paper)
ISBN-10 0-252-03306-X (cloth : alk. paper)
ISBN-13 978-0-252-07508-7 (pbk. : alk. paper)
ISBN-10 0-252-07508-0 (pbk. : alk. paper)
1. Schrader, Paul, 1946—Criticism and interpretation.
I. Title.
PN1998.3.S358K68   2008
791.4302'33092—dc22   2007037242

Contents |

"You want to hear a personal story? Okay, I'll tell you a personal story—not about me, of course. About my grandfather, Carter Page the First." So begins one of the strangest moments in Paul Schrader's *The Walker* (2007). The person telling the story is Carter Page III (Woody Harrelson), the film's central character. Car, as the women in his canasta circle refer to him, is a part-time real estate agent and full-time gossip. He earns his place at the canasta table by regaling the women with amusing stories about the private lives of the Washington political elite and by escorting them to various art openings and society functions. At these events, Car's homosexuality is an open secret. Out of deference to the distinguished political careers forged by his father and grandfather, the Washington establishment tolerates his presence. If it hasn't become apparent already, Car is the most recent installment of a character type that traverses Schrader's body of work: the loner or peeper who drifts through life looking at a world of relationships, emotions, and human engagements on the other side of the glass. At each phase of Schrader's career, this character type has been accompanied by a particular mood: anger, narcissism, anxiousness, or fear of the future. In *The Walker,* the dominant mood is one that Schrader charted early in his directorial career: a sense of superficiality or an attitude that nothing really matters. At the end of the film, this sense of superficiality is replaced by a more somber yet also more hopeful recognition of one's capacity to change and take oneself by surprise.

Car's story concerns his grandfather when he was a young man and his love affair with a woman in a photograph, Johanna Combs of Philadelphia. For a year, the grandfather corresponded daily with Johanna, writing letters in which his longing is conveyed in the type of prose that, as Car quips, reads as if it were written by "a man with a Bible half-open in his head." After a year of corresponding, the grandfather caught the train to Philadelphia. That night, he and Johanna attended the opera. During the intermission, Carter Page I rose from his seat and returned home to the family estate in Covesville, Virginia. The grandfather and Johanna never saw each other again. As a footnote to the story, Car reveals that when his grandfather and the woman who became his grandmother had their first child, a daughter, she was named Johanna.

"And that's it?" asks Car's listener. "That's the story?" "That's all I ever heard." After a pause, he adds, "I'd give my right arm to know the rest of it." Our first response to this shaggy-dog story is to wonder why it has been included in the film: basic information about the love affair is missing. Yet the more we think about this story, the more it typifies Schrader's career. His films are about characters ruled by forces and impulses that remain a profound mystery both to themselves and others. The stories told about these characters often don't cohere or resolve in a traditional sense. Who is to say why Car's grandfather abandons his first love or why he holds on to her memory to such an extent that he names his firstborn in her honor? Despite this lack of explanation, these stories exercise a powerful fascination. The gaps and missing pieces of information suggest the presence of compulsions and drives that can never be approached directly, but only glanced in their often violent or self-destructive aftereffects.

For the past four decades, Schrader has made a career out of tracing these aftereffects. The stories in his films are underpinned by a sense of existential mystery and a belief that, no matter how much we may assume otherwise, we can never really know what it is that drives or leads us to take certain decisions and actions. So single-minded has Schrader been in his approach to this fundamental scenario that, across his films, we often witness the replaying of not only character types but also certain shots, camera movements, and stylistic allusions. This repetition creates a body of work in which the obsessions and impulses that drive the characters also mark the filmmaker's own relationship to his work. Schrader's willingness to put himself in the picture has often led to a blurring of the lines between filmmaker and character, a process that the director's own comments have tended to encourage. It has also fostered an impression that Schrader tacitly endorses the often difficult and antisocial behavior of his characters. Bound up in the rage and drive to self-realization of the characters, critics argue, is the director's own identity. As we shall see, disentangling the nature of Schrader's commitment to his characters—separating the teller from the tale—represents only one of the challenges posed by his films.

The writing of this book owes a lot to the contributions of a number of key individuals. My friend and colleague, James Donald, helped set up the correspondence between Jim Naremore, the series editor, and myself. At all times, Jim has been a model of diligence and support. In 2005 I spent a couple of days at the offices of Schrader Productions; the interview with the director occurred during this time. Schrader was remarkably frank and open to all questions raised. Once the interview was concluded, he was kind enough to allow me to peruse his personal files and correspondence going back many years. The stories and personal histories contained in these files will one day surely become the subject of a much larger and more extensive account of Schrader's history and role in contemporary Hollywood. My time at Schrader Productions would not have been as fruitful without the help and good humor of Schrader's assistant, Tony Mosher. Tony provided access to images, tapes of interviews, and scripts. I also had to call on Tony's services during the copyediting stage. In Sydney, Effie Rassos was a wonderful research assistant. She also transcribed the interview and put together the bibliography and filmography. Working with Effie has been a highlight of not only this book but also a number of other projects. Finally, I want to thank my partner, Janice Zwierzynski, and daughter, Gena Kouvaros, for their many years of patience, support, and love.

The Teller and the Tale |
The Films of Paul Schrader

All my life, the moment any idea occurs to me the opposing idea
occurs with equal force. It's why I can never really make anything
that's settled, because I just have always found that contradictory
ideas exist quite well in my head.

—Paul Schrader, *The South Bank Show*

Near the end of *Mishima: A Life in Four Chapters* (1985), the troubled author reflects on the possibility of a higher principle where art and action are reconciled: "To survive in this atmosphere, man, like an actor, must wear a mask." This comment brings the film back full circle to the events of November 25, 1970: the day when, along with four members of his private militia, the Shield Society, Yukio Mishima (Ken Ogata) took over the offices of the commander of the Eastern Army Headquarters. The opening moments detail the commencement of this day: Mishima waking, shaving, drinking coffee, and reading the newspaper. Each activity seems to carry the weight of a larger purpose that drives the protagonist and the film forward. For Mishima, the activity that holds greatest significance involves the process of putting on the dress uniform of the Shield Society. After laying the uniform on the bed, he takes a few small steps back to admire its beauty. We have seen these actions before in another film directed by Paul Schrader. In *American Gigolo* (1980), Julian Kay (Richard Gere) prepares to meet one of his clients by laying on his bed a choice of clothes. The admiring glance down at the bed and the camera pan left to right are here as well. But this time the accompaniment is Smokey Robinson and the Miracles rather than the militaristic drumbeat of Philip Glass's *Mishima* score.

Beyond the sense that both Mishima and Julian are fashioning uniforms, Schrader's filming of the preparations implies a deeper connection between the two films. The meticulous manner in which these characters prepare to dress suggests not only a state of heightened self-consciousness but also a desire to re-create the self through the perfecting of certain roles. This desire links Mishima to Julian and also to Travis Bickle (Robert De Niro) from *Taxi Driver* (1976). For Travis, the struggle with roles is part of a desperate attempt to achieve human engagement. Whether he is standing in front of the mirror perfecting his gunplay or gazing at the crowds of people that pass his cab, Travis is, all the while, looking for a way to break free of the isolation and terrible loneliness that define his relationship to the world.

Over the years, Schrader's own identity has become closely linked with his troubled characters. Richard Combs describes Schrader as "the poet laureate of the type: the crazed outsider who doesn't shun the system so much as long to create a finer, purer, nobler one—one created, in fact, in his own image" (Combs, Review of *Mishima* 300). Two decades on from the publication of these remarks, Schrader's films represent one of the most interesting examples of a body of work that is resolutely grounded in mainstream commercial filmmaking yet also driven by ideas and influences that work against commercial imperatives. This duality is what makes films like *Light Sleeper* (1992), *Affliction* (1997), and *Auto Focus* (2002) interesting, yet it also poses a challenge for critics looking to pin the films down as either commercial or experimental, mainstream or independent.

Something similar characterizes the career of Schrader's former collaborator, Martin Scorsese. As is the case with Schrader's films, Scorsese's work exemplifies what Adrian Martin characterizes as authorial "indirectness." "In Scorsese's films," writes Martin, "the 'real' story, the one which drives and generates everything we see and hear, is hidden, camouflaged, displaced. It is the very definition of his art and craft as a practicing filmmaker that he finds, in whatever project is presented to him, the 'secret' element that will make it truly his" (Martin, "Fuck

Him" 148). The identification of this secret element passing between each of Scorsese's films is one of the mainstays of film publishing.

Schrader's films are also driven by a similar set of obsessions. But whereas Scorsese's work has attracted a vast body of critical writing, Schrader remains on the margins of critical debate. One reason for this is that Schrader's reputation is based as much on his achievements as a screenwriter—*The Yakuza* (1975), *Taxi Driver, Obsession* (1976), *Rolling Thunder* (1977), *Old Boyfriends* (1979), *Raging Bull* (1980), *The Mosquito Coast* (1986), *The Last Temptation of Christ* (1988), *City Hall* (1996), and *Bringing Out the Dead* (1999)—as it is on his work as a director. And because the most critically lauded of these scripts have been for films directed by Scorsese, there is a tendency to treat Schrader's work as a subset of the work of his better-known and more stylistically flamboyant collaborator. The partnership between Scorsese and Schrader produced *Taxi Driver, Raging Bull, The Last Temptation of Christ,* and *Bringing Out the Dead.* It also set up an automatic point of comparison. Lorraine Mortimer exemplifies this approach: "*American Gigolo,* if appealing, does not come close to the vibrancy of a Scorsese film. It is more purely a Protestant story with its sensuous charge coming primarily from its music, its photographed beautiful objects, cars, clothes, furnishings, and Julian in his 'unwired' beauty" (Mortimer, "Blood Brothers" 33).

Mortimer's comments also illustrate the tendency of critics to weave into their analysis references to Schrader's religious upbringing. Time and again, Schrader's strict Calvinist upbringing in Grand Rapids, Michigan, is used to explain the style and confrontational content of his films. For his part, Schrader has obliged critics by providing a series of linkages between the films and formative events in his personal life—a capacity, no doubt, honed through his own activities as a critic. Few critics could match Schrader's acute discussions of not only the strengths and weaknesses of his own films but also their defining influences. The danger is that in trying to do justice to Schrader's own comments, it is possible to limit what can be said about the films. Yet to ignore these comments runs an even greater risk of failing to recognize the contradictory energies, impulses, and ideas that drive his films.

Dana Polan makes the salient point: "No matter how sophisticated auteurism becomes under the influence of new approaches from theory and history, it is still about persons and their fates and destinies" (Polan). The interesting thing about Schrader is the difficult nature of this personhood. He is too visible, commenting on and analyzing his films in advance of the critic, yet not visible enough—lacking in visual flamboyance or distinctive style. His films are driven by a highly personal and idiosyncratic set of ideas and principles and mainstream commercial formulas.

Coinciding with these tensions between private obsessions and commercial formulas is a recurring theme concerning self-realization. To borrow a memorable line from *Taxi Driver*, in Schrader's films, to "become a person like other people" is no easy task. This is why those moments of dressing that link *Mishima* and *American Gigolo* are so highly charged. The pleasure taken in the uniform carries with it the echo of an inevitable resistance that cannot be overcome or mastered. "I've always been interested in people," Schrader observes, "perfectly intelligent people, who seem to have some sort of grasp on life but go around acting in a self-defeating way because they are expressing some neurosis—either sexual or spiritual" (Kaplan 35). Closely shadowing the various neuroses and hangups of Schrader's characters is an equally powerful sense of estrangement, of meanings and things just out of reach. Even characters as resolutely superficial as Julian in *American Gigolo* or Bob Crane (Greg Kinnear) in *Auto Focus* or Carter Page in *The Walker* find themselves struggling to comprehend social worlds that have changed and left them behind. "All your life, you're the lucky guy, the funny guy," muses Crane. "Then one day it all turns: the jokes aren't funny; the phone doesn't ring. You're the same, but nothing else is."

This sense of social exclusion feeds into self-defeating behavior. It also keeps Schrader's protagonists at a distance from our attempts at identification. Neil Sinyard claims that the heroes in Schrader's films "are not anguished idealists or angry young men. They are heroes who challenge any attempt at identification or moral approval. . . . They reflect a contemporary confusion and skepticism about heroism and modern heroes and their morality is personal, private and idiosyncratic" (Sinyard 514). This study will consider how Schrader's skepticism about heroism connects his films to a broader context of American filmmaking in the 1970s. The tensions and contradictions evident in Schrader's films— between old and new ways of telling a story, between the maintenance of commercial formulas and an openness to personal expression—mirror the tensions and contradictions that characterized the American cinema during this period.

Schrader's authorship of the screenplay to *Taxi Driver* and the success of *American Gigolo* positioned him at the forefront of a new generation of American writer-directors. Yet the same qualities that made these films successful—Schrader's commitment to pursuing the extreme aspects of his characters' behavior, his embrace of contradictory styles and filmic traditions—ultimately meant that his career would pursue its own idiosyncratic course. For Schrader, the act of cinematic storytelling has its roots in a deeply personal need to understand oneself and one's relation to others. "I reached a point when non-fiction wasn't doing the trick," Schrader explains in a discussion of the factors motivating his shift from critic to screenwriter. "I had emotional needs that demanded to be fantasized, to be acted out. They needed characters, they had to come alive. . . . So I came into filmmaking for all the best reasons. You can discharge these angry feelings in a healthy context" (Rechler 31). Over the years, Schrader has achieved a safe distance from the agonies of his early protagonists. Despite this mellowing, it is hard to imagine another filmmaker capable of making a film as corrosive about American male identity as *Auto Focus* or as invested in the transforming potential of romantic love as *Forever Mine* (1999). Both films are expressions of the obsessive tendencies and contradictions that continue to motivate Schrader's approach to cinema.

The image of Schrader's films driving this commentary is of a body of work marked by different genres, styles, and collaborative engagements. Holding this varied body of work together is, as I have suggested, a concern with the possibilities of self-realization. Far from being unique, this theme forms one of the central pillars of American literature and film. Schrader's treatment differs from the traditional renderings of this theme in that the restless searching of his protagonists does not lead to the reaffirmation of a larger communal or family group. The view of the world presented in Schrader's films is essentially that of an outsider. In the interview following this commentary, Schrader describes this outsider figure as "The Peeper, The Wanderer, The Voyeur, The Loner," whose origins can be traced to Schrader's own experience of "coming from a rather strict background and then being confronted with L.A. circa 1968. And that sense of the push-pull, the sense that you can't stop looking, but you can't get inside the room either." Finding a way in for this character has not been easy. Each phase of Schrader's career has brought with it new emotions as well as new challenges. Running through these changes and developments is an ever-present sense of the instability of social networks, a sense that it is possible to wake one morning and, like Crane or Julian or Carter Page, find that it has all turned.

These themes will govern my choice of films and screenplays. I will concentrate on those films where the contradictory impulses that drive Schrader's characters have achieved the greatest resonance for audiences and the filmmaker. In the interview, Schrader takes up some of the issues raised in the commentary. His remarks also touch on more general matters to do with cinema's changing place within media culture and the necessity of the canon in the study of film. The range of topics covered gives some sense of Schrader's concerns about cinema and contemporary culture. The interview took place in New York over two days in September 2005. Just prior to the interview, Schrader had secured funding for *The Walker* and was negotiating the casting of the lead role. In the period leading up to the interview, he had also agreed to direct an adaptation of a novel by the Israeli writer Yoram Kaniuk, *Adam Resurrected*. When we sat down to commence the discussion, Schrader's office was full of books, DVDs, and tapes used as research for a study on the film canon that he had agreed to write for Faber and Faber.[1] Given this range of commitments, Schrader's willingness to schedule time to be interviewed was extraordinarily generous and indicative of the importance he places on cinema as an arena for ideas and critical discussion.

The New Hollywood

At the midpoint of the 1970s, Thomas Elsaesser identified an important change in the representation of the male hero.[2] While the protagonists in films such as *Two-Lane Blacktop* (1971), *Five Easy Pieces* (1970), *The Last Detail* (1973), and *California Split* (1974) share attributes with their classical counterparts, their behavior is disconnected from a motivating context: "[T]he significant feature of this new cinema," Elsaesser proposes, "is that it makes an issue of the motives—or lack of them—in its heroes" (Elsaesser, "Pathos" 280). This undermining of motivation gives rise to a dramaturgy quite distinct from that found in classical Hollywood narrative:

> [C]lassical narrative was essentially based on a dramaturgy of intrigue and strongly accentuated plot, which managed to transform spatial and temporal sequence into consequence, into a continuum of cause and effect. The image or scene not only pointed forward and backward to what had been and what was to come, but also helped to develop a motivational logic that functioned as an implicit causality, enveloping the hero and connecting him to his world. . . . Out of conflict, contradiction and contingency the narrative generated order, linearity, and articulated energy. (280)

The motivation connecting the hero to his world provides the narrative with direction and shape: "Contradictions were resolved and obstacles overcome by having them played out in dramatic-dynamic terms or by personal initiative: whatever the problem, one could do something about it, and even eventually solve it" (281). In films such as those cited above, contradictions and obstacles are no longer amenable to the application of personal initiative. This is evidenced by changes in the journey. In these films, the journey goes nowhere: "Taking to the road comes to stand for the very quality of contingency, and a film like *Two-Lane Blacktop* is symptomatic in this respect: there is only the merest shadow of an intrigue, the action provocatively avoids the interpersonal conflicts potentially inherent both in the triangular relationship and in the challenge personified by the Warren Oates character" (281). This development can be traced back to the work of an earlier generation of directors, in particular, Robert Aldrich and Sam Peckinpah. Elsaesser describes *Bring Me the Head of Alfredo Garcia* (1974) as a "study . . . of a hero who has no past to romanticize (as in *The Wild Bunch* [1969], or *Junior Bonner* [1972]) and who is thus more radically unmotivated than any previous Peckinpah character" (284).

Elsaesser's comments provide a valuable overview of changes within the American cinema during the 1970s, but it is not clear how closely Schrader's films relate to these changes. The striking thing about characters such as Travis in *Taxi Driver* and Jake VanDorn (George C. Scott) in *Hardcore* (1978) is not their lack of motivation but rather their deeply contradictory nature. Both characters serve as spokesmen for traditional values and relationships, yet they both end up in the role of violent vigilante. Such a contradiction is not unusual in the American cinema. Schrader's work differs in the extent to which he keeps these contradictory elements dangerously alive. In so doing, he places the audience in a difficult position: How much sympathy should we have for these characters? How much should we identify with their actions? What judgment should we make? And as a filmmaker, Schrader is as torn as his audience. He is fascinated and repelled by the behavior of his characters.

The larger question shadowing Elsaesser's analysis has direct relevance to Schrader's work: How far is it possible to consider the New Hollywood cinema as experimental? Elsaesser claims that the answer to this "comes down to how the skepticism about motives and justification in the hero, and the doubt about an experience of social and political life . . . are translated into a formal search for a film narrative free from the parasitic and synthetic causality of a dramaturgy of external conflict" (Elsaesser, "Pathos" 283). After surveying the work of various American directors, Elsaesser sees cause for optimism. He notes that the appeal to the spectator's emotional identification in *Thieves Like Us* (1974) or *The Sugarland Express* (1974) enables a cautious attempt to cope with the problem of "how to depict the unmotivated hero." Elsaesser concludes that while European directors such as Jean-Marie Straub, Jacques Rivette, and Luis Buñuel "can work at purely situational narratives . . . in the comforting knowledge of an appreciative intellectual audience," the pressures on such experimentation in Hollywood cinema mean that American directors pursue a more familiar course: "Consequently, the innovatory line in the American cinema can be seen to progress not via conceptual abstraction but by shifting and modifying traditional genres and themes, while never quite shedding their support, be it to facilitate recognition or for structuring the narrative" (287).

The shifting and modifying of traditional genres is an essential part of Schrader's work. Starting with the coauthored Japanese gangster script *The Yakuza*, Schrader has found ways to accommodate the idiosyncrasies and obsessions that define his central characters within popular generic formulas. *Blue Collar* (1978), for example, uses the framework of the caper film to tell a story of claustrophobia and alienation. In *Taxi Driver* and *Hardcore*, Schrader draws on the iconography of the Western to explore the darker impulses of male heroism. *Mishima, Patty Hearst* (1988), and *Auto Focus* address the challenge of telling the life story of protagonists whose personal histories are constructed around a series of irreconcilable performances and masks. Perhaps Schrader's most audacious reworking of genre occurs in *Cat People* (1982): a loose remake of the 1943 horror classic by Jacques Tourneur in which the founding premise of the earlier film, concerning an ancient race of people able to move between human and animal form, is used to explore a drama about sexual awakening and self-realization.

Schrader's career bears out the fact that, in the 1970s and 1980s, genre filmmaking flourished because it could accommodate the experimental impulses of the new generation of American directors and the need of the studios to offer easily recognizable narrative formulas. In commercial terms, the strategy of revising traditional formulas can be linked to a period of industry crisis at the start of the 1970s. "For the American film industry," David A. Cook observes, "the 1970s began in a state of dislocation matched only by the coming of sound. The recession of 1969 had produced more than $200 million in losses; left MGM, Warner Bros., and United Artists under new management; and brought Universal and Columbia close to liquidation" (Cook, *Lost Illusions* 9). Cook lists as reasons for this crisis a string of expensive commercial failures between 1966 and 1968, a national recession, record-high interest rates of around 10 percent, and the emergence of smaller companies that had achieved the status of mini-majors by distributing foreign and independent production. The modest success of youth-oriented films like *Bonnie and Clyde* (1967), *The Graduate* (1967), and *Easy Rider* (1969) could not prevent the fall into recession, but it did help create the conditions necessary for a new generation of directors to gain entry into mainstream Hollywood filmmaking.

One of the things that distinguished this new generation of filmmakers from previous generations was its high degree of film literacy. In part, this can be attributed to the impact of television. Not only did television provide a constant supply of film product, it also served to generate its own version of recycled genre parodies in various sitcoms and nightly dramas. Robert B. Ray claims that television's plundering of Hollywood's past "encouraged a new attitude toward the popular cinema and the traditional mythology it embodied" (Ray 264). The other factor to be considered is the rise of film-study courses across U.S. campuses. Cook notes that in 1967 "there were approximately 1,500 film and television courses being offered at 200 colleges, and these numbers would quintuple over the next ten years" (Cook, *Lost Illusions* 69).

The way in which this film literacy affected the films produced has attracted significant critical attention. Noël Carroll provides the most scathing account of this phenomenon. Surveying a range of films, Carroll identifies a tendency among new filmmakers to allude to the work of canonical directors. In Carroll's argument, allusion covers a range of different practices: "[Q]uotations, the memorialization of past genres, the reworking of past genres, *homages,* and the recreation of 'classic' scenes, shots, plot motifs, lines of dialogue, themes, gestures, and so forth from film history" (Carroll 52). Carroll describes the outcome of this varied practice as "a two-tiered system of communication which sends an action/drama/fantasy-packed message to one segment of the audience and an additional hermetic, camouflaged, and recondite one to another" (56). This practice of double layering "presumes an extremely knowledgeable spectator who will interpret the new film—the reworking—against a backdrop of the accepted associations of the appropriate genre. That is, the reworking evokes a historical genre and its associated myths, commonplaces, and meanings in order to generate expression through the friction between the old and the new" (57).

Whether or not one agrees with Carroll's overall assessment of the implications of such a practice, it is important to acknowledge the extent to which it plays a part in Schrader's films. Scattered through his films are allusions to the work of canonical directors such as Robert Bresson, John Ford, Alfred Hitchcock, Michelangelo Antonioni, and Bernardo Bertolucci. As Carroll rightly points out, for Schrader, as for others of his generation, allusion is not an end in itself but a way of marking one's place within an ongoing history of formal and thematic exploration whose terms are set in advance. I differ from Carroll in attributing the significance of such a practice to not only the points of similarity but also the variegation and difference between old and new. Schrader uses a deliberate practice of allusion—to his own films as well as the films of others—as a way of working through problems and issues that lie at the heart of his troubled protagonists and their relationships to the world at large.

The final factor to be considered when reviewing changes in American cinema at the time of Schrader's emergence is the abandonment of the Motion Picture Production Code and the implementation of a ratings system in 1968. The introduction of ratings provided a mechanism by which producers were able to negotiate for the inclusion of content that would otherwise have been deemed unacceptable by the industry (Cook, *Lost Illusions* 70–71). Coupled with the commercial success of genre reworkings such as *The Wild Bunch* and *Bonnie and Clyde*, these changes in industry, audience, and films helped create the ambivalent phenomenon of formal experimentation working in tandem with traditional paradigms and formulas. Schrader's films—their generic allegiances and contradictory characters—are a prime example of this ambivalent phenomenon.

From Grand Rapids to Hollywood

Schrader's emergence as a filmmaker shares characteristics with others of his generation: for example, a highly refined film literacy developed through its formal academic study and a capacity to rework traditional genres and forms. But it is also distinguished by important differences. Compared to others of his generation, Schrader's immersion in film came late. The fundamental details of Schrader's upbringing in a devout Dutch Calvinist family in Grand Rapids are well known. His family's adherence to a 1928 synod decree warning against the dangers of "worldly amusements" meant that activities such as going to the movies were proscribed. In his extended interviews with Kevin Jackson, Schrader describes the excitement of sneaking into a movie theater at the age of seventeen to see *The Absent-Minded Professor* (1963) and his subsequent disappointment at the film's failure to live up to his mother's warnings (Schrader, *Schrader on Schrader* 5).[3] It was only after viewing the more libidinously charged *Wild in the Country* (1961), starring Elvis Presley and Tuesday Weld, that Schrader came to understand his mother's concerns.

Originally intending to pursue a career as a minister, Schrader enrolled at Calvin College to study theology and liberal arts. During his time at Calvin, his interests in literature and writing merged with a newfound passion for film. Schrader's involvement in running the college's film society and writing on film for the school newspaper led him to spend a summer at New York's Columbia University studying film on a more formal basis. Part of this adventure involved a meeting with the influential critic Pauline Kael. An invitation to dinner turned into an all-night discussion about the relative merits of different films: "[T]he conversation just went on all night long, with real arguments—I liked the films she didn't like and vice versa—and I ended up sleeping on her couch. The next morning as I left she said to me, 'You don't want to be a minister—you want to be a film critic'" (*SOS* 15).

After returning to Calvin College, Schrader kept in contact with Kael. This friendship was crucial in his decision to apply to UCLA's film program. Schrader commenced his studies at UCLA in the fall of 1968, and at this point his personal history starts to resemble those of his generation of American directors, whose coming of age involved a passionate engagement with the history of cinema:

> When I came to UCLA I had a lot of opinions about film but not a great deal of information. I just hadn't seen that many movies. So I devoted my first two years in L.A. to seeing films, plain and simple. . . . All I did was see films and keep a log. At the end of the first year I went through the log and found that I'd been seeing twenty or twenty-five films a week, scuttling back and forth to all the various film societies and educating myself in my future profession of critic. As soon as I had cleaned up the European cinema, which was my first love, I got on to the American cinema, the [Andrew] Sarris canon, and cleaned that up. (*SOS* 20–21)

This relentless pursuit of film history links Schrader to others of his generation. The fact that it came relatively late, however, has important consequences: "I find myself alone among my colleagues in not having childhood memories of movies to fall back on. My childhood memories revolve around theological discussions at the kitchen table, around religious proselytizing. There are no movie memories, period" (*SOS* 21). While this may have put Schrader at a disadvantage in terms of the viewing histories of his fellow directors, it also meant that he was able to draw on a distinct set of experiences for his films: "It just didn't matter to me how successful my friends were because I wasn't making their kind of movies and they weren't making mine. I never felt that internecine rivalry because, say, Walter Hill would go off and make his John Ford film whereas I would go off and make my Grand Rapids film" (*SOS* 21).

When Schrader sums up how his background affected his view of film, he describes the formation of "an intellectual's perception of mass entertainment as opposed to a child's" (SOS 21). Elsewhere, he elaborates on the implications of this perception of film: "Film for me is not the least bit nostalgic. I see film simply as a tool at my disposal—the most accessible artistic medium I could use" (Bragg, South Bank). These remarks help clarify a number of important points. For Schrader, the experience of cinema proved so powerful because it formed an extension of the world of ideas and religious debate central to his family background in the Christian Reform church. The hours spent sitting around the dining table participating in religious discussions instilled a sensibility in which cinema is a vehicle for ideas. Schrader's willingness to take on risky projects and not be daunted by an apparent lack of cinematic potential is a direct consequence of this sensibility. Over and above a film's value as cinema lies its intellectual challenge: How do I tell this story? What approach could do justice to the issues and characters involved? The director's eclectic style—its mixing of traditional formulas and more overtly experimental tendencies—was formed in response to these questions.

While studying at UCLA, Schrader began work as a critic, first for the L.A. Free Press and then Cinema, a journal he took over and edited. His writings range from an iconoclastic critique of Easy Rider, extended considerations of Bresson's Pickpocket (1959), studies of Hollywood directors such as Budd Boetticher and Sam Peckinpah, and an influential survey of the elements that define film noir. Commenting on the range of film styles and issues covered in Schrader's writings, Kevin Jackson sees clear hints as to his future inclinations as a director: "Schrader was drawn, on the one hand, to the intellectual detachment of La Prise de Pouvoir par Louis XIV [1966] (judged by most critics at the time to be 'cold' and 'boring'); on the other, to The Wild Bunch, a film which 'uses violence to excite and then applies more violence to comment on the excitement.' Might not an attempted synthesis of these seemingly contrary approaches look very like a Schrader film?" (qtd. in SOS 33–34).

As he was finishing his studies at UCLA while working as a professional critic, Schrader began writing a book that was to become Transcendental Style in Film: Ozu, Bresson, Dreyer. This book was completed after

Schrader graduated from UCLA and had commenced an appointment as a fellow at the American Film Institute's Center for Advanced Film Study. As defined by Schrader, "Transcendental style seeks to maximize the mystery of existence; it eschews all conventional interpretations of reality: realism, naturalism, psychologism, romanticism, expressionism, impressionism, and, finally, rationalism" (Schrader, *Transcendental* 10). The filmmakers at the heart of his investigation—Yasujiro Ozu, Robert Bresson, and Carl Dryer—belong to a tradition of art cinema working in opposition to dominant styles of commercial filmmaking, in particular, the emotional associations that underpin the operations of character. "The whole of the *Transcendental Style* hypothesis," Schrader explains, "is that if you reduce your sensual awareness rigorously and for long enough, the inner need will explode and it will be pure because it will not have been siphoned off by easy or exploitative identifications" (*SOS* 28).

A number of critics have found ways of explaining the nature of Schrader's films within the book's central thesis. For his part, Schrader has been careful to distinguish his practice of filmmaking from the austere work of those directors who are part of a transcendental tradition. "The reason why I don't make transcendental films . . . is that I believe in something that is anathema or contrary to the whole notion of transcendental cinema. I have my roots in psychological realism and audience identification with character, whereas the whole notion of transcendental style is based on repudiating psychological realism" (Bliss 9). The interesting thing about Schrader's relation to transcendental filmmaking is the way it highlights not clear-cut affiliations or rejections but the coexistence of contradictory and opposing tendencies. While in some discussions he sets his work apart from the rigor of transcendentalism, at other times he acknowledges points of contact:

> One of the things that I've tried to do in my films . . . is to try to have an emotionally blinding moment, like Mishima's suicide; or like the end of *American Gigolo,* where this spiritual essence suddenly pops out of the flimsy lounge lizard; or like the moment in *Light of Day* [1987] when the girl is reconciled with her mother, where, despite all her toughness, she can't deny any more that there is something which transcends you, and that the more you suppress it the more it's going to knock you on your ass. (*SOS* 29)

These remarks do not solve the question of whether or not Schrader is a transcendental filmmaker, but they allow us to recognize the coexistence of competing sensibilities and traditions: moments of austere transcendentalism working hand in hand with Hollywood's need for emotional involvement. Bill Nichols sums this point up nicely: "[W]hat is most intriguing is not the possibility of placing Schrader squarely in either camp, but of teasing out the (contradictory) tension between material conditions and transcendental resolutions to which he gives compelling expression" (Nichols 13). Nichols leaves open the question of how far a connection between Schrader the writer and Schrader the filmmaker can be pursued. In a postscript to Nichols's article, Schrader also allows the question to stand: "I have chosen to believe that my current work as a writer and director and my previous work as a critic have nothing in common. This doesn't mean they have nothing in common; it means I've chosen to believe they don't" (13).

Picking up on the competing influences that drive his films, Elsaesser identifies Schrader as part of what he terms a "European crossover" in American cinema that takes the form of a strong stylistic influence and desire for a highly personalized approach to filmmaking. According to Elsaesser, the careers of directors such as Schrader undo simplistic oppositions between art and commerce while also providing "a model for a third possibility: that art and commerce are always in communication with each other" (Elsaesser, "American" 67). This third possibility suggests that the American cinema of the 1970s is best understood "not so much as a period either of radical innovation or of mere transition, but of crossovers, which is to say, shifts that mix the meaning of signs in order to make all kinds of slippages . . . both possible and functional" (67).

Whatever way we look at this period in American film, Schrader's career stands as one of its most remarkable outcomes: an intellectual working in the midst of Hollywood's rampant commercialism; an American director influenced by European cinematic traditions; an iconoclast whose films and scripts keep open the possibility of spiritual redemption. While these crossovers can help us to identify some of the contradictory forces at work in Schrader's career, their true value may lie in withholding a unitary critical perspective. Rather than being a problem for Schrader, one suspects, this is precisely what allows his work to remain open to the possibility of discovery—personal and filmic. The challenge for criticism is to track this movement of discovery or productive change.

The Lure of Negative Thought: *Taxi Driver*

Schrader's experience in crossover filmmaking began with his efforts to secure financing for his first script, "The Pipeliner"—the outcome of an attempt to produce a script that could be filmed for less than one hundred thousand dollars while also adhering to a transcendental structure (Thompson 8). Although he was unsuccessful, the experience proved invaluable: "I had a good look at the denizens of the deep that inhabit film financing and the next time around I was much more savvy about why people put up money for films, which is an important part of being a film-maker" (*SOS* 111). At the same time, a dispute with the head of the American Film Institute (AFI), George Stevens, resulted in Schrader's departure from his position as fellow. This event coincided with a number of other personal crises that eventually led to what has become the defining event of his creative career: "I was out of work; I was out of the AFI; I was in debt. I fell into a period of real isolation, living more or less in my car. A grim time. And out of that isolation came *Taxi Driver*, which was written in just ten days; the first draft was about seven and the rewrite was three. It just jumped out of my head like an animal" (*SOS* 111).

Schrader sent the script to his agent; he also showed it to Brian De Palma, who brought it to the attention of the producers Julia and Michael Phillips. Through their recommendation, the script was passed on to Martin Scorsese and Robert De Niro. Despite Scorsese's immediate enthusiasm for the project, the lack of commercial clout of those involved meant it was to be another two years before conditions were in place to begin production. After writing *Taxi Driver*, Schrader began a period of drifting around the country. His fortunes changed dramatically when he received a letter from his brother, Leonard, who was working in Kyoto as a missionary: "My brother had fallen on hard times himself and his marriage had also broken up. He had taken to watching lots of Japanese gangster movies. So I called up my agent friend in L.A. and said, 'I've had this fascinating letter from my brother. I think that it might be a very commercial idea to do a Yakuza film, a kind of Japanese version of the Kung-fu films'" (*SOS* 113).

Schrader's hunch proved accurate. Coauthored with Leonard, *The Yakuza* became the subject of a bidding war. The script sold for $325,000, an extraordinary sum at the time. It was eventually directed by Sydney Pollack and released in 1975. Invigorated by this success, Schrader began work on a number of other projects—one of which was the screenplay entitled "Déjà Vu," which De Palma eventually made as *Obsession*. The turning point came when finance was secured to produce *Taxi Driver*.

The controversy surrounding *Taxi Driver* has never left Schrader's career. The immediate influence for the script and character of Travis Bickle was Jean-Paul Sartre's *Nausea*. "Travis's is not a societally imposed loneliness or rage," Schrader explains, "it's an existential kind of rage" (*SOS* 116). For most critics, it is not the connection to European existentialism that provides the defining context for the film. Far more frequently cited is Schrader's account of his own personal circumstances: "At the time I wrote it I was very enamored of guns, I was very suicidal, I was drinking heavily, I was obsessed with pornography in the way a lonely person is, and all those elements are upfront in the script. Obviously some aspects are heightened—the racism of the character, the sexism" (*SOS* 117).

On its release, influential critics such as Pauline Kael, Vincent Canby, and Andrew Sarris praised *Taxi Driver*. It was also awarded the Palme d'Or at the 1976 Cannes Film Festival. Costing around $1.9 million to produce, the film's initial gross was about $17 million. As Amy Taubin points out, *Taxi Driver*'s cultural impact far exceeds its commercial success:

> An enigma and a piece of common knowledge, Travis Bickle is lodged in the collective cultural consciousness to a degree that makes an aesthetic evaluation of *Taxi Driver* almost irrelevant. As in a hall of mirrors, Travis's fetishised reflection within the film is projected onto the world outside and back again, ad infinitum. The answer to critics who find *Taxi Driver*'s open ending dubious on both moral and logical grounds is what has happened in the near twenty-five years since the film's release. (Taubin 75)

Criticism of the film concentrates on two issues. The first concerns its combination of stylistic allusions to art-house cinema auteurs and commercially driven exploitation techniques. Patricia Patterson and Manny Farber describe *Taxi Driver* as "a half-half movie: half of it is a skimpy story line with muddled motivation about the way an under-educated misfit would act, and the other half is a clever, confusing, hypnotic sell" (Patterson and Farber 29). Travis's racism has also come under stinging criticism. Quoting from interviews given at the time of *Taxi Driver*'s release, Jonathan Rosenbaum claims that Schrader's "degree of moral conflict and confusion—no doubt stemming in part from Schrader's strict Calvinist upbringing—seems to border at times on the pathological" (Rosenbaum 150). According to Rosenbaum, this pathological mindset lies at the heart of the film's troubling appeal to audiences: "[T]he audience is invited to identify with a violently Calvinist, racist, sexist, and apocalyptic wish-fulfilment fantasy, complete with an extended bloodbath, that is given all the allure of expressionist art and involves very few moral consequences for most members of the audience" (151).

Schrader does not deny the racist nature of the central character: "There's no doubt that Travis is a racist. He's full of anger and he directs his anger at people who are just a little lower on the totem pole than he is" (qtd. in Taubin 16–17). Schrader draws a distinction, however, "between making a movie about a racist and making a racist movie": "I love to make movies about people who are disapproved of by society because I feel if you can get people to identify with a character they don't think is worthy of identification, then you open them up in some way and who knows what happens once they open up" (17). Elsewhere, he is more explicit about the value of the audience's identification with the central character: "I think one is stung into progressive, positive behaviour by an awareness of the great lure of negative thought; it's the awareness of prejudice inside you that spurs you on to rid yourself and others of it" (*SOS* 117).

Looking over the screenplays and films that follow the release of *Taxi Driver*, Schrader's comment on the lure of negative thought provides a useful point of connection. Julian, Jake La Motta, Mishima, Patty Hearst, and, more recently, Bob Crane: each is a rendition of character in the negative. Each lacks the moral coherence we look for in central characters. In *Taxi Driver*, Travis rails against the scum and filth of the streets; but he spends a large portion of his time in porn theaters. He primly lectures Iris (Jodie Foster): "You're a young girl, you should be at home now. You should be dressed up. You should be going out with boys. You should be going to school. You know, that kinda stuff." In the next breath, he accuses her of selling her "little pussy for nothing . . . for some lowlife pimp . . . who stands in the hall."[4] He chastizes himself for his unhealthy lifestyle, yet he continues to pop pills and pour apricot brandy on his breakfast cereal. For Schrader, these inconsistencies and contradictions are central to Travis's "self-imposed loneliness":

> When I set out to write the script I thought it was about loneliness. As I wrote it I realized it was about something a little different but more interesting, which was self-imposed loneliness: that is, a syndrome of behavior that reinforces itself. And the touchstones of that kind of behavior are all kinds of contradictory impulses: Puritanism and pornography at the same time; "I've got to get healthy" while popping pills at the same time. That dreadful diet. It's all full of these things that he does to make sure he'll never get to where he's going. In other words, so he can reinforce his own doomed condition. (Bouzereau)

For Robin Wood, these contradictions point to a deeper incoherence. In Wood's estimation, *Taxi Driver*—like *Cruising* (1980) and *Looking for Mr. Goodbar* (1977)—typifies a range of films where "the drive toward the ordering of experience has been visibly defeated" (Wood 42). The mixed messages in these films are the result of the demise of Classical Hollywood narrative and the cultural and political upheavals of the 1960s and 1970s: "Society appeared to be in a state of advanced disintegration, yet there was no serious possibility of the emergence of a coherent and comprehensive alternative. This quandary . . . can be felt to underlie most of the important American films of the late 60s and 70s" (44). In the case of *Taxi Driver*, this situation is exacerbated by a "relatively clear-cut" conflict between the film's two auteurs: the "liberal humanist" Scorsese and the "quasi-Fascist" Schrader (45). In fact, Wood's purpose is not to delve into the politics of Schrader's films. It is, rather, to provide an explanation—in the form of a critical straw man—for *Taxi Driver*'s unresolved contradictions and darker political leanings, the key manifestation of which is the central character:

Travis' behavior is presented as increasingly pathological (culminating in his acquisition of a Mohawk Indian haircut), with his ambitions increasingly monstrous (the assassination of a politician no worse than most) and his achievements useless, unless one has an automatic commitment to the family. . . . [T]he film can neither clearly reject him (he remains, somehow, The Hero . . .) nor structure a complex but coherent attitude to him (such as [Michael] Cimino partially achieves in *The Deer Hunter* [1978]). (47–48)

Despite his gestures towards moral uncertainty, Wood's notion of the incoherent text relies on the moral authority of the critic to disentangle good from bad, progressive from reactionary. If the reams of critical writing inspired by *Taxi Driver* have proven anything it is that this sort of elevated critical practice differs significantly from the way audiences actually engage with the film. As Schrader has reiterated in numerous interviews, his intention in *Taxi Driver* was not to simply condemn Travis's behavior but to engage the audience in its dangerous pull. This does not mean that Schrader's approach to cinema is, as Wood proposes, "quasi-Fascist." Rather, it is based on a deliberate undermining of moral certainty. Travis is both a hero and a psychopath, a rescuer and a deluded killer.

Taubin provides a broader contextualization of Travis's alienation. She reads the film as a reworking of the Western—in its classical form in films like *Shane* (1953) and its revisionist manifestations in films like *The Wild Bunch*. *Taxi Driver* shares with these films a critical relation to a history of American male violence: "Walking towards us on 57th St., which in the early morning is as empty as a Texas prairie, Travis is carrying the centuries of American history written in blood. His claim to have served in the Vietnam War may or may not be true. But it is not Vietnam alone that produced him. He is the product, rather, of the repetitive cycles of violence that have made the United States number one" (Taubin 37). Lesley Stern also locates Travis's pathology in terms of a repetitive enactment of male violence that links broader political events like the Vietnam War and specific cultural representations such as Ethan Edwards (John Wayne) from John Ford's *The Searchers* (1956): "Both Ethan Edwards and Travis Bickle have returned from war, having fought on the losing or retreating side. For both of them the dividing line between war and peace is a wavering line" (Stern 57). Stern goes on to describe Travis as "a mixture of urban cowboy and Vietnam vet—he wears rider jeans, cowboy boots, a plaid Western shirt and a worn beige army jacket with a patch reading 'King Kong Company, 1968–1970'" (57).

Operating alongside these cultural influences and allusions is another set of influences drawn from Schrader's critical writings. In Schrader's study of Bresson's films, he notes that the alienated protagonists "are condemned to estrangement: nothing on earth will placate their inner passion, because their passion does not come from earth" (Schrader, *Transcendental* 76). In *Taxi Driver*, the source of Travis's estrangement is more earthbound. Hence, its stylistic leanings veer more toward the individualized agonies of melodrama than the austere transcendental style of Bresson. *Taxi Driver* seems closest to Bresson in its use of voice-over narration to articulate what Schrader terms "disparity." "All my life needed," Travis writes in his diary, "was a sense of someplace to go. I don't believe that one should devote his life to morbid self-attention. I believe that someone should become a person like other people." Travis's musings and self-admonitions in his spoken diary entries intensify

Taxi Driver: Travis (Robert De Niro) is both a hero and a psychopath, both a rescuer and a deluded killer.

our engagement with the central character while also emphasizing his disconnection from the world at large. Writing things down doesn't help Travis. The close-ups of the half-finished sentences render thought visible not as a pretext for action but as the outcome of affective overload. All these words on paper, bumper stickers, and humorous wall mottos—"One of these days, I'm gonna get organiz-ized!"—chart not a way forward but exacerbate the sense of chaos and crackup.

The Psychopath's Second Coming

During the writing of *Taxi Driver,* Schrader learned the important trick of creating the sense of things happening without purpose or direction while offering just enough in the way of plot: "Plot is tricky in character studies. Ideally they should be plotless, dwelling on the complexities and contradictions of human behavior, guiding the viewer to one of several conclusions. That's unrealistic in the commercial cinema. The trick is to have just enough plot so that it seems like something is happening, but not so much that the viewer thinks it's about plot" (Schrader, *Collected* viii). Viewed through the distorted lens of the cab's windshield, the activities of the city appear as a series of random encounters without context or explanation: a group of kids emerge from a side street and toss eggs at the car; a man walks down the street screaming, "When I get my hands on her, I'll kill her! I'll kill that fucking bitch!" The twelve-hour shifts, headaches, and lingering insomnia have left Travis unable to register things properly. Even when he is taking a break with the other cabbies, Travis is ill at ease and slightly removed from the conversation. Patterson and Farber define Travis's sense of remove as a question of social power and belonging:

> A chief mechanism of the script is power: how people either fit or don't fit into the givens of their status, and the power they get from being socially snug. Travis's dream girl has power because she has a certain golden beauty and doesn't question or rebel against her face or her position as political campaigner. . . . The cabbies, more or less at peace with themselves, are glimpsed as a gang not fighting job or status. The movie shows the facts of being in or out. Everyone plays this power game but Travis—he can't figure what kind of game he wants to play. (Patterson and Farber 29)

When Travis attempts to enter the game—to "become a person like other people"—his efforts inevitably go wrong. He becomes infatuated with Betsy (Cybill Shepherd), a campaign worker for Senator Charles Palantine (Leonard Harris). He sits in his cab outside her office and watches her—as Cynthia Fuchs notes, in much the same way that he watches the screen in the porn theatres (Fuchs 705). Travis cleans himself up, strides into the campaign offices, and volunteers his services. When he confesses to Betsy that his real reason for volunteering is to take her out for coffee and pie, she is curious enough to agree. Over coffee, Travis asks Betsy if she likes her work and the guy she works with. "His energy seems to go in the wrong places," he tells her. Travis explains that he can tell that there is "no connection" between Betsy and her colleague. A short time later, Travis returns to his potential rival: "That fella you work with, I don't like him. It's not that I don't like him . . . I just think he's silly. I don't think he respects you." Betsy is not quite sure how to take Travis's strange pronouncements. When she compares him to a character in a Kris Kristofferson song—"He's a prophet and a pusher, partly truth, partly fiction, a walking contradiction"—Travis takes her comments literally: "I'm no pusher. I never have pushed."

Whether it is because he completely misreads Betsy or because he secretly wants to sabotage the potential relationship, the next time they go out, Travis takes her to a porn film. When Betsy balks at the choice of movies, he tells her: "No, no, this is a movie that a lot of couples come to. All kinds of couples go here." Schrader's script fills in part of the explanation for Travis's behavior: "He is so much a part of his own world, he fails to comprehend another's world. . . . But then there's also something that Travis could not even acknowledge, much less admit: that he really wants to get this pure white girl into that dark porno theatre" (Schrader, *Collected* 48). In *Taxi Driver* and elsewhere in Schrader's work, affection and hostility work hand in hand. Travis's self-loathing and underlying puritanical streak mean that any form of sexual expression is clouded by violence—directed at either himself or others. This deadly combination is central to the now-infamous scene that occurs just after Travis's disastrous date with Betsy. Travis picks up a male customer, played by Scorsese himself, who asks him to pull up outside of an apartment building. On the seventh floor, the outline of a woman's body can be seen in the window. "That's my wife," explains

Taxi Driver: Betsy (Cybill Shepherd) and Travis, once again at cross-purposes.

the customer. "But that's not my apartment." He then proceeds to bait Travis with his murderous thoughts: "Did you ever see . . . did you ever see what a .44 magnum pistol can do to a woman's face? I mean, it can fucking destroy it. Just blow it right apart. That's what I can do to her face. Now, did you ever see what it can do to a woman's pussy? *That* you should see. That you should see, what a .44 magnum's gonna do to a woman's pussy, you should see." Coming from just behind Travis's head, the jealous customer's voice turns the cab into an echo chamber where Travis's own fears and anxieties gather force and take on a grotesque dimension.

The misunderstandings that characterize Travis's encounter with Betsy are replayed with Iris, a young prostitute he first meets one evening when she jumps into the back of his cab. Before Travis is able to drive off, her pimp, Sport (Harvey Keitel), drags Iris out of the cab. Travis is convinced that Iris is being held against her will. When he tracks her down, he tries to get Iris to remember the encounter in the cab: "But *you're* the one that came into my cab. *You're* the one that wanted to get out of here. God damn it, don't you want to get out of here?" Despite having his assumptions shot down, Travis arranges to meet Iris again the next day. He tries to convince her to go back to her family in Pittsburgh. When he tells Iris that Sport is a killer, she replies: "Sport never killed no one. . . . He's a Libra." Near the end of their conversation, Travis tells Iris that he'll give her the money to get home, but because he has something important to do she may not see him for a while.

Taxi Driver: After being rejected by Betsy, Travis switches his attention to Iris (Jodie Foster).

The thing Travis has to do is get revenge on Betsy and, by implication, all the others who have consigned him to the status of a nobody. It is hard to tell how long this plan has been brewing—at least since he purchased the cache of firearms and decided to get in shape, or perhaps even earlier, when Senator Palantine stepped into his cab. Travis rigs up a metal glider that will release a small .38 handgun from its hiding spot into his palm. He also implements a process of bodily purification that involves holding his arm over the flame of a stove. When the assassination attempt on Palantine is foiled, Travis sets off to rescue Iris and commits the bloody slaughter that has become his hallmark.

From one perspective, the bloody slaughter is randomly motivated. From another perspective, it is the logical outcome of everything that has happened to Travis. "It is the release of all that cumulative pressure," writes Schrader. "It is the psychopath's Second Coming" (Schrader, *Collected* 116). After Travis runs out of bullets, he collapses onto a red velvet sofa. A group of cops rush the room. As Travis stares back at the cops, he forms his hand into the shape of a pistol, lifts it to his head, and makes the sound of a gun firing. Schrader's script specifies not only the way the conclusion of this shocking scene should be filmed but also exactly what should be shown during the camera's slow exit. The elongated sentence structure conveys a sense of unrelenting carnage:

> Live sound ceases. Overhead slow-motion tracking shot surveys the damage: from Iris shaking against the blood-spattered wall; to Travis's blood-soaked body lying on the sofa; to the old man with half a head, a bloody stump for one hand, and a knife sticking out of the other; to police officers staring in amazement; to the private cop's bullet-ridden face trapped near the doorway; to puddles of blood and a lonely .44 Magnum lying on the hallway carpet; down the blood-speckled stairs on which lies a nickel-plated .38 Smith and Wesson Special; to the foot of the stairs where Sport's body is hunched over a pool of blood and a small .32 lies near his hand; to crowds huddled around the doorway, held back by police officers; past red flashing lights, running policemen and parked police cars; to the ongoing nightlife of the Lower East Side, curious but basically unconcerned, looking then heading its own way. (Schrader, *Collected* 115–16)

As specified in the script, Scorsese shoots all of this in a series of extremely high-angle slow-motion tracking shots that move from inside the blood-soaked apartment, back out along the corridor, down the stairs, and finally to the street outside. This sequence echoes the overhead tracking shot away from the murder scene in Hitchcock's *Frenzy* (1972). But whereas in *Frenzy* the camera's exit from the building seems to erase the crime, in *Taxi Driver* the long slow track back over the bodies, pools of blood, and abandoned weapons highlights the full extent of Travis's crime. It also removes the audience from the point of view of the protagonist by relocating them above the scene.

In Schrader's discussion of Bresson, he evokes the idea of a "decisive action": an action that is the culmination of the protagonist's dilemma as well as its transformation: "In *Diary of a Country Priest* [1950] the decisive action is the priest's death, when his frail body falls from the frame and the camera holds on a blatant symbol: the shadow of the cross cast on a wall. In *A Man Escaped* [1956] it is the nocturnal escape, with its concomitant and all-important acceptance of grace in the person of Jost" (Schrader, *Transcendental* 79). The implications of the decisive action bear as much on the spectator as they do on the protagonist: "The decisive action forces the viewer into the confrontation with the Wholly Other he would normally avoid" (81). In Bresson, this involves an acceptance or rejection of spiritual grace. In *Taxi Driver*, the decisive action brings us face to face with the culmination of Travis's alienated rage. From this point on in the film, we continue to see Travis, but we no longer hear from him in the same way.

The sense of having broken away from the protagonist is confirmed when the film cuts from outside the building where the slaughter occurs to another tracking shot inside Travis's apartment. Some time has passed. This is conveyed by the newspaper articles about Travis's crime stuck on the wall: "Taxi Driver Battles Gangsters"; "Reported New York Mafioso Killed in Bizarre Shooting"; "Parents Express Shock, Gratitude"; "Taxi Driver Hero to Recover." As the camera surveys these headlines, an older male voice on the soundtrack reads a letter sent to Travis by Iris's parents. The fact that this voice does not belong to Travis is more of a shock than Travis's reincarnation as a hero. No longer an anonymous nobody, for a while at least, he's somebody. Even Betsy returns to Travis when she appears in the back of his cab and asks how he's doing. Wood criticizes the film's conclusion for leaving open the suggestion that Travis has achieved "some kind of personal grace or existential self-definition"

(Wood 48). Such a suggestion can only be maintained by ignoring the overt irony of Travis's elevation to the status of hero and the film's conscious disengagement from his perspective.

The final touch in the film belongs to Scorsese, but it sums up the disturbance at the heart of Schrader's script. On three occasions during Travis's encounter with Betsy, his eyes appear in the rearview mirror. On each occasion, Scorsese's filming suggests that Travis is looking not only at what is happening in the back seat but also at himself. The final time is after Betsy gets out of the cab and Travis starts to drive away. This time, Travis seems to catch himself off-guard. In a strangely speeded-up motion, he does a double take and looks back at the mirror. It's as if what he catches sight of is not himself but a stranger. In the years following, each of Schrader's protagonists will, in one way or another, replay this encounter with the stranger's face: a vision of themselves not as themselves but as other.

From Screenwriter to Director: *Blue Collar* and *Hardcore*

The period of *Taxi Driver*'s production coincided with the writing of a number of other screenplays. In the space of a few years, Schrader had an uncredited early role in the script for Steven Spielberg's *Close Encounters of the Third Kind* (1977), cowrote with Heywood Gould the script for *Rolling Thunder*, and embarked on his second collaboration with Leonard on the script for Joan Tewkesbury's *Old Boyfriends*. In a survey article published in *American Film*, Bruce Cook summed up Schrader's place in the industry: "Although Paul Schrader has yet to prove himself as a director, there can be little doubt that he has established himself as a true auteur-screenwriter, perhaps the only one around" (Cook, "Talents" 60). Sinyard provides a more impressionistic summation: "[I]t is tempting to think of Schrader and Scorsese's floating yellow taxi-cab (in the first shot of *Taxi Driver*) and Spielberg's floating yellow spacecraft (in *Close Encounters*) as the two most resonant emblems of the decade. They represent the extremes of menace and magic that were Hollywood's chief box-office assets during the turbulent 1970s" (Sinyard 514).

At the time, Schrader's motivation for this prolific output was to build his commercial value to the point where he could offer a script for free on the condition that he would be given the chance to direct. Moving into direction was the only way Schrader could gain artistic control of his work: "[I]f you want to be in control of what you are doing as a writer you either have to become a novelist like Gore Vidal or John Gregory Dunne or you have to get into directing. Being a screenwriter is in the end rather unsatisfying for an artist. It's very satisfying commercially and it's a pleasant lifestyle, but in the end you don't really feel you have anything that represents you" (*SOS* 141).

The outcome of this strategy was Schrader's first film as a director, *Blue Collar*: a story about three Detroit automotive workers. Frustrated by the difficulty of making ends meet, Zeke Brown (Richard Pryor), Smokey James (Yaphet Kotto), and Jerry Bartowski (Harvey Keitel) decide to rob their local union office. During the robbery, the three friends discover a notebook listing a series of illegal loans to New York and Las Vegas business interests. Unsure about how to deal with their discovery, Zeke and Jerry are persuaded by Smokey to use the notebook as a way of blackmailing the union. Rather than caving in to their demands, the union buys Zeke's loyalty by offering him the job of shop steward. Shortly after this, Smokey is killed in a suspicious workplace accident. Terrified that he might end up like Smokey, Jerry agrees to testify against the union.

Despite the political connotations of its storyline, Schrader describes the film's politics as "the politics of resentment and claustrophobia, the feeling of being manipulated and not in control of your life" (*SOS* 148). These feelings also form the basis of Travis's self-imposed loneliness in *Taxi Driver.* In both films, this sense of claustrophobia and lack of control gives rise to self-destructive behavior: "I wanted to write a movie about some guys who rip off their union because it seemed to me such a wonderfully self-hating kind of act, that they would attack the organization that's supposed to help them" (Crowdus and Georgakas 34).

Blue Collar differs from *Taxi Driver* in the way that it links this self-destructive behavior to the social realities governing the working lives of the three friends: poorly paid, monotonous labour, hostile bosses, as well as personalized aggravations such as a locker that remains broken for six months or the inability to pay for a child's braces. The barroom camaraderie and late-night cocaine parties organized by Smokey, the only bachelor in the group, serve as refuge from the drudgery. But these activities are underpinned by an ever-present sense of individual frustration. As Jerry rues at the tail end of one of these evenings: "Every time I get coked up like this, I think I'm never going to go back to the plant. I don't know why the fuck I do."

A key factor in the film's treatment of the frustrations driving the robbery and the downfall of the three friends—two of whom are black and the other white—is the issue of race. When Zeke decides to accept the union's offer to become shop steward, Jerry accuses him of being bought off. Zeke's response emphasizes the fundamental difference between the two men:

> ZEKE: You're my friend, Jerry, but you're thinking white.
> JERRY: What the fuck does that mean?
> ZEKE: It means that you got more chances than I got, Jerry . . . and you're always gonna have more chances than me. I got one chance, and I'm gonna take it. I'm black, Jerry; the police ain't gonna protect me.

In the final scene, Jerry returns to the factory accompanied by government agents. As he is leaving, Zeke confronts Jerry, and the former

Blue Collar: Smokey (Yaphet Kotto), Jerry (Harvey Keitel), and Zeke (Richard Pryor), struggling with the aftermath of one of their late-night parties.

friends turn on each other in a tirade of racist insults. The final shot is a freeze frame of Zeke and Jerry at the point of physical confrontation. Over the top of this image, Schrader replays Smokey's earlier grim summation of the politics of resentment fostered at the plant: "They pit the lifers against the new boy, the young against the old, the black against the white. Everything they do is to keep us in our place."

Schrader's next film, *Hardcore,* provides a template for much of the work to follow by narrowing its examination of alienated male behavior to a single individual: Jake VanDorn, whose runaway daughter has become involved in the world of pornography. Schrader describes *Hardcore* as one of two "more or less autobiographical films": "*Hardcore,* which is about my father, and *Light of Day,* which is about my mother—and I think they both may have failed commercially because they're a little too personal" (*SOS* 149). In his discussions with Jackson, Schrader expresses dissatisfaction with the film's moral contrast between the rectitude of VanDorn and the depravity of the pornographers. The other element Schrader finds disappointing is the way the ending succumbs to the traditional Hollywood imperative to reconcile father and daughter: "Originally I had the daughter being killed in a car accident, or in some way completely unrelated to pornography, so the father goes on this kind of journey through hell seeking to redeem his daughter, finds out that she has been killed in some mundane way and then has to go home and live with what he's learned" (151).

Despite Schrader's disappointment, *Hardcore* clarifies a number of directorial touchstones. It begins with a series of shots of the snow-covered streets and houses of Grand Rapids. A similar snowbound existence is evoked at the start of *Affliction.* In both films, Schrader foregrounds a sense of place as a way of making visible a type of behavior. This interest in place and behavior runs through a number of other films, including *American Gigolo, Light of Day,* and *Light Sleeper.* In each of these films, Schrader creates a drama that is individualized and linked to a general context. Based on his upbringing in the tight-knit Calvinist community of Grand Rapids, the context evoked at the start of *Hardcore* is one the director knows particularly well. This familiarity is suggested in the lyrics of the country and western hymn sung by Susan Raye: "Precious memories, unseen angels, sent from somewhere to my soul." We get a better sense of the lives and behavior of the people occupying this place when the film cuts to a house full of the rituals and social activities of Christmas: while their parents discuss theology, bored children and teenagers stare blankly at dreadful holiday television specials.

VanDorn and his daughter, Kristen (Ilah Davis), are part of this community. But the absence of VanDorn's wife sets them apart. This absence may also explain the awkwardness and formality that characterize VanDorn's interactions with his daughter. This sense of estrangement comes to the fore when Kristen goes missing at a Calvinist youth convention. Frustrated by the police department's limited resources, VanDorn hires a private detective (Peter Boyle) to track her down. A few weeks later, the detective presents him with evidence that Kristen has become involved in the world of pornography. He warns VanDorn: "There's a lot of strange things happen in this world. Things you don't know about in Grand Rapids. Things you don't wanna know about. Doors that shouldn't open." These doors that shouldn't open lead VanDorn away from his home and to Los Angeles, where he encounters a world that his life in Grand Rapids has left him ill-equipped to comprehend.

VanDorn's efforts to trace his daughter start producing results when he poses as a wealthy businessman interested in financing a porn film. This disguise provides him with access to a previously closed world; it also exacts a high price. The first time he sees Kristen on screen, Jake averts his eyes and screams for the film to stop. Over the course of the film, he becomes more immune to these sorts of images. In *Hardcore*, the challenge faced by VanDorn is not only to find Kristen; it is also to reconcile his actions and experiences with the values of the community he leaves behind. That these things are irreconcilable is a suggestion the film—even with its contrived resolution—can't completely shake off.

The prototype for this drama of irreconcilability and internal conflict is Ethan's quest to rescue his kidnapped niece in *The Searchers.* Schrader acknowledges the influence of this film on *Hardcore* and *Taxi Driver.* Discussing the reasons for the film's importance—not only in his own work but in the work of a whole generation of American filmmakers—Schrader describes Ethan as "a man who is deprived of the pleasures of hearth and home because he has blood on his hands. At the end of the movie he walks away and the door closes on him; he has returned the lost child to the home but he can't enter" (*SOS* 155). Ethan's savagery places him beyond the reach of home. When, after seven long years of wandering,

Hardcore: Jake's (George C. Scott) response to
witnessing his daughter in a porn film.

his obsessive journey ends, Ethan heads back to the wilderness: a dark
embodiment of the violence that underpins the Western hero.

Characters like VanDorn continue along this path. So too does Travis
and less well-known figures like the Vietnam veteran Charles Rane (William Devane) in the script for *Rolling Thunder*. After spending seven
years in a prison camp in Vietnam, Rane returns home to find his wife
about to marry his best friend. Rane's life is dramatically transformed
by a violent home invasion that results in the mutilation of his hand and
the death of his wife and child. After recovering, Rane sets off to find
his family's killers. In the original version of the screenplay for *Rolling
Thunder*, the central character was very much in the mold of Travis: "The
character, as I originally wrote him, was a Texas trash racist who had
become a war hero without ever having fired a gun, and came home to
confront the Texas Mexican community. All his racism from his childhood and Vietnam comes out, and at the ending of the film there's an
indiscriminate slaughter of Mexicans, meant as some kind of metaphor
for American racism in Vietnam" (*SOS* 121).

The only way to get *Rolling Thunder* made was to remove the overt racism of the central character—"which is the equivalent of giving Travis Bickle a dog" (*SOS* 121). While *Hardcore* does not contain the blood-thirsty elements of either *Taxi Driver* or *Rolling Thunder,* it evidences a similar struggle over how far to go in its undermining of the male hero. VanDorn wanders through a world he barely understands; yet his efforts to extract information on his daughter's whereabouts highlight a clear tendency to violence. He even turns on Niki (Season Hubley), the young prostitute who helps him in his quest. As is the case in *The Searchers,* the further VanDorn travels, the more his actions undermine the things he hopes to affirm. When VanDorn finally locates his daughter, her first response highlights the falsehood of his quest: "They didn't make me do anything . . . I wanted to leave." At the end of *Hardcore,* VanDorn's tears, like those of Howard Kemp (James Stewart) in *The Naked Spur* (1953), make clear that the central point of the journey was not to retrieve the lost daughter but to expose the frailty of the male hero.

Hardcore: George C. Scott, Paul Schrader, and Season Hubley, who plays Niki, prepare to shoot a scene on location in San Diego.

Hardcore thus helps to clarify one face of alienation in Schrader's films: the quest-driven obsessive whose attempt to make things right inevitably brings with it a violent outcome. Read accordingly, VanDorn looks back to Travis in *Taxi Driver* and Rane in *Rolling Thunder* while also looking forward to Wade Whitehouse's (Nick Nolte) desperate attempt to get to the bottom of things in *Affliction*. To varying degrees, each of these characters has blood on his hands. The precedents for this tale can be found in films like *The Searchers*, but also in the work of Hitchcock. Schrader rewrites Hitchcock's most famous tale of male obsession, *Vertigo* (1958), in the script "Déjà Vu," which was filmed by Brian De Palma as *Obsession*. At the start of *Obsession*, Michael Courtland (Cliff Robertson) witnesses the death of his wife and child in a bungled kidnapping. Grief-stricken, Michael builds a shrine to their memory. When the film jumps forward sixteen years, Michael returns to the Florentine church where he first met his wife. While walking through the church, he is struck by the resemblance between his late wife and a young woman, Sandra Portinari (Genevieve Bujold), working on the restoration of the church's art works. Later, we discover that Sandra is the daughter Michael believed had died many years earlier in the botched kidnapping.

As in *Vertigo*, Michael has been set up by a friend. Yet, on another level, it is clear that he is the victim of his own incapacity. In *Vertigo*, John "Scottie" Ferguson's (James Stewart) fear of heights and guilt at not being able to prevent Madeleine Elster's (Kim Novak) death are merely the obvious manifestations of an underlying pathology that drives him further and further into a state of deadly obsession. Likewise, in *Obsession*, Michael's incapacity seems to stem not only from his deep feelings of guilt about the part he played in the death of his wife and child but also from an underlying psychic crisis. Near the start of the film, Michael is feted by his friend and business partner as "a man of endless energy and ambition." These words deliberately echo those of Scottie's chief tormentor in *Vertigo*, Gavin Elster (Tom Helmore), who longs for the "power" and "freedom" enjoyed by the industrial elite of old San Franscisco. In *Obsession* it is the failure of this power and freedom as much as the loss of his wife and child that throws Michael into crisis. The appearance of his wife's lookalike offers him a second chance. He brings Sandra back to New Orleans, and arrangements are made for a wedding. But replaying the past does not bring with it mastery or healing. It recommences a demonic pattern whereby things that have happened before happen once again.

Near the end of *Obsession*, Michael's tormentor looks down and sneers: "You just can't seem to keep a woman, can you?" This taunt could be leveled at a number of Schrader's protagonists. His films not only return to and consciously replay moments that highlight the failure of American heroism but also imbue this failure with an overtly sexual dimension. Like Scottie in *Vertigo*, Michael's desire to "keep a woman" stands in for a fundamental incapacity that he is unable to contemplate directly. And like Scottie, at the very moment Michael thinks he has achieved control, he finds that others have, once again, controlled him.

In "Déjà Vu," Schrader continues the story of Michael's obsession into the 1980s. This third act was to provide one more turn of the screw that would confirm the story's vertiginous structure. Although Schrader was unable to convince De Palma to stick with the original ending, the impossibility of resolving the scenario of male obsession is evidenced in the way Schrader's films keep returning to this issue. In this sense, his films are not just about obsession; they enact the very thing they wish to represent. They *obsess*. Instead of being debilitating, Schrader's enactment of this crisis serves as the impetus for an important recasting of the American cinema.

A Man and His Room: *American Gigolo*

Just as the scenario explored in *Hardcore* crystallizes themes found in a number of other films, *American Gigolo* also has a defining role. As well as attracting an enormous amount of critical attention—positive and negative—the film achieved significant commercial success. Coming directly after *Blue Collar* and *Hardcore*, Schrader regarded *American Gigolo* as his last chance to make an impact as a director: "*American Gigolo* was the third script I had stacked up ready to direct. I wanted to build a career and I wanted to have at least three shots from the gun before they took it away from me" (*SOS* 157). One reason for *American Gigolo*'s impact was its controversial content. This time the controversy centered not on the depiction of violence but the film's treatment of sex. Like Hal Ashby's *Shampoo* (1975), *American Gigolo* caused a stir

American Gigolo: A widely circulated publicity still of Richard Gere as Julian Kay. This image highlights the film's framing of Julian as object of display and its highly stylized use of lighting.

because its exploration of sex focused not on an eroticized female character but on a new kind of male performer whose sexual identity is overtly on display.

Schrader describes the theme of *American Gigolo* as "the inability to express love." The metaphor used to articulate this theme is the life of a gigolo: "I realized that the character of the gigolo was essentially a character of surfaces; therefore the movie had to be about surfaces, and you had to create a new kind of Los Angeles to reflect this new kind of protagonist" (*SOS* 158). To create the new version of Los Angeles, Schrader drew on the talents of the German composer Giorgio Moroder for the music, Giorgio Armani for the costumes, and the Italian production designer Ferdinando Scarfiotti to provide an overall design concept. Scarfiotti's highly stylized use of color and design in Bertolucci's *The Conformist* (1970) had made a strong impression on Schrader: "*The Conformist* was a very important film for my generation, because it was a film that reintroduced the concept of high style. Movies used to have high style in the thirties and forties and then gradually, through the fifties and sixties, they became more realistic, less production-designed, and *The Conformist* became a real sort of rallying cry" (*SOS* 160).

In *American Gigolo*, the employment of high style is evident in its carefully coordinated pastel tones, the décor of the apartments, and the choice of locations. The film treats its highly stylized settings as a means of defining the central character's identity. At the start of the film, at least, the central character is one more object in a world full of objects to be admired, gazed upon, and purchased. Sharon Willis argues that the film "is explicitly structured around the male body as a feminized display. . . . The story of the gigolo's being falsely accused of the rape and murder of a client entails the unraveling of his pose, and his position in the world, where he circulates in high-class circles—hotels, clubs, art galleries—and the implicit threat of a social fall back into the world of the streets and gay discos" (Willis 55). Willis concludes that Julian's increasingly desperate efforts to clear himself of the crime are an attempt to "ward off feminization." These comments sum up an interpretive thread running through a number of discussions of the film.[5] The issue I want to consider proceeds along a slightly different line: How does this presentation of Julian link him to other characters in Schrader's films and, in particular, the model of obsession identified in *Hardcore, Taxi Driver,* and *Obsession?*

One of the first things registered in the film are the opening notes of Blondie's "Call Me." The song reaches full pitch when a close-up of a shiny chrome wheel traveling at speed replaces the plain black background of the initial credits. This shot is quickly replaced by another close-up of a car's taillight. The different positions occupied by the camera across the cut create the impression that the car is traveling in two directions at once. The car's occupant is revealed in a high-angle traveling shot that frames a black Mercedes convertible. The close-up shots of the car and Julian's glance into the rearview mirror recall the opening of *Taxi Driver*. But *Taxi Driver* and *American Gigolo* couldn't be more different in their depiction of the milieu occupied by the central character. During the opening moments of *Taxi Driver*, Travis's cab emerges out of a dense cloud of steam that, as Taubin observes, "suggests that what we're about to see is some kind of hybrid of an urban horror film, an urban road movie and a psychodrama with neo-noir overtones" (Taubin 34). Through the windshield of the cab, the city's inhabitants are barely distinguishable blurs of color moving in a type of hypnotic trance.

Instead of this suffocating nightscape of slow-moving bodies and urban congestion, *American Gigolo* locates its protagonist in a space defined by speed and unhindered movement. The thrill of traveling alongside the convertible while listening to Blondie positions the film somewhere between a music video and a large-budget commercial. This impression is reinforced when the car pulls up in front of Juschi, a luxurious Beverly Hills boutique. We watch Julian nonchalantly pass the keys to the valet and enter the boutique. The film then cuts to a shot of the protagonist standing in front of a mirror getting fitted for a suit. When we next pick up Julian, he is admiring his new acquisition near a register. Once again, the shot is from a high angle. In the background of the shot, a woman who was previously helping Julian select a tie for his suit is at the register paying. Another quick cut shifts the location to outside a suburban house. Julian is with the same woman. But rather than entering the house, he kisses her at the door and gets back into the car. The next shot returns Julian to where we first found him: unhindered and alone on the highway.

All through this opening sequence, lasting just over three minutes, the camera positions Julian as central to the story, but its constant motion and rapid cutting implies something unknowable about him. Commenting on the film's opening, Peter Fraser describes Julian as "an object of curiosity and desire, but never a knowable human being" (Fraser 95). During the opening moments, his identity shifts from the confident operator shown in the credits to the polite, almost nervous, chauffeur who gradually wears down the defensiveness of his out-of-town client. Both roles are equally valid. Although the endpoint of each performance is always predetermined, Julian's talent resides in his ability to keep this masked. Everything in this world is about sex. But what Julian has learnt is the importance of keeping this disguised or unspoken.

In this world of surfaces and carefully rehearsed seductions, the only time we get close to Julian is when he is in his apartment. This is where Julian prepares for his clients. These preparations involve choosing the right clothes but also more arduous tasks, such as hanging by his feet from an exercise bar while listening to Swedish phrases from a Berlitz tape. Julian's attempt to learn Swedish is part of how he gets ready to meet an overseas client. On a more general level, it indicates a degree of preparation and training that he applies to all aspects of his life. Julian's commitment to training and bettering himself reminds us of Travis's belated efforts to put his life in order. For both characters, these acts of self-creation evoke a sense of isolation and loneliness that is just under the surface.

In large measure, Schrader draws his inspiration for Travis and Julian from Bresson's *Pickpocket*. In his rundown one-room apartment, Michel (Martin LaSalle), the central character in Bresson's film, trains his hands to memorize the supple movements and actions necessary to be a successful pickpocket. Michel's pickpocketing has what Schrader calls a "familiar obsessive quality; it is neither sociologically nor financially motivated, but instead is a Will to Pickpocket" (Schrader, *Transcendental* 77). Michel justifies his actions by believing in the innate right of certain special individuals to exist beyond the rules of ordinary men. In *American Gigolo*, Schrader replays this credo when Detective Sunday (Hector Elizondo) asks Julian if he is bothered by the fact that what he does is illegal. Julian replies: "Legal is not always right. Men make laws, sometimes they're wrong . . . or stupid. Or jealous. . . . Some people are above the law." As in *Pickpocket*, this moment highlights how far the protagonist has gone in the pursuit of an ideal and how far he has to fall.

This is the other face of male obsession in Schrader's films. Borrowing directly from a European tradition of existentialism exemplified not only by Bresson but also Fyodor Dostoevsky, Albert Camus, and Jean-Paul Sartre, films like *American Gigolo, Taxi Driver,* and *Mishima* represent Schrader's "man and his room" stories (*SOS* 163). These films are less task driven than the stories in *Hardcore* or *Rolling Thunder.* They center on individuals whose isolation is driven either by paranoia, as in *Taxi Driver,* or by the obsessive pursuit of an ideal, as in *American Gigolo* and *Mishima.* Schrader's representation of obsession differs from that of his European counterparts in its overt connection to sexual anxiety. As Willis rightly notes, in *American Gigolo* this is manifested in Julian's attempts to deal with his loss of status and the threat of falling back into the world of male tricks. Willis's term for this is "feminization," but the underlying issue is the same as in *Taxi Driver, Blue Collar, Obsession,* and *The Walker*: an anxiety about social power and belonging, or, as Patterson and Farber put it, "the facts of being in or out." In one way or another, the loss of social power drives the desperate actions of Schrader's characters.

For all his poise and careful preparation, Julian is blind to his place within a larger social network; it is left to other characters to fill him in. "You're just a hanger-on," he is told by Michelle's husband. "You live off the good graces of a small number of people." Julian's retainer, Leon Jaimes (Bill Duke), puts it even more bluntly: "Nobody *cared* about you. I never liked you much myself." These words cut Julian down to size, but they also remind us that his fate in the film is to be acted on by others. Just as he is set up for a murder he didn't commit, Julian achieves redemption not through his own doing but by accepting Michelle Statton's (Lauren Hutton) love. Julian's predicament evokes a situation that will become clearer as Schrader's career unfolds: finding one's sense of identity taken over by an external force. In the films to come, Schrader keeps returning to the dangers and attractions of such a subjective takeover.

In *American Gigolo,* the compromised nature of Julian's carefully fashioned existence is exemplified during his fateful encounter with the Rheimans. Although they are outside his regular circle of clients, Julian takes the job—in part as a favor to Leon, and in part because he can squeeze Leon out of his usual cut. When he arrives at the house he discovers that, instead of his usual arrangement, he will have to deal with a couple. He attempts to assure Mrs. Rheiman (Patti Carr), who is lying naked in the bed, that nothing bad will happen, but his routine is interrupted by the directions of her husband: "No, no, no. From behind! It has to be from behind!" The morning after his encounter with the Rheimans, Julian meets with Leon. Still bristling from Julian's hard bargaining, Leon provides a frank assessment of how little control Julian actually has over his own destiny: "You know, you walk an awful thin line, Julie. I wouldn't want to be in your shoes. I mean, you're getting awful cocky. All the rest of the boys are happy with a car, a house in the hills. But not you. You got all your rich pussy lined up. Once-a-month tricks. A dip in the pool, a little tennis, an orgasm. I'm just trying to warn you as a friend: those bitches ever turn on you, you're through."

Leon's warning signals the end point of Julian's journey, but questions remain: Who will turn on Julian? And will he be able to recognize the threat? The difficulty Julian faces is that the signs of his downfall and the possibility of redemption emerge almost simultaneously. When Julian first encounters Michelle in a bar, he mistakes her for a wealthy French tourist. On discovering that she is in fact the wife of a local politician, Julian pulls back. His real mistake is to assume that Michelle is unaware of what he is: "How much would you have charged me?" she asks. "As what? A translator . . . or a guide?" he replies. Michelle's response is to the point: "No. Just one fuck." Is Michelle's blunt response a case of Julian being feminized? Or is it one more example of his carefully guarded poise and control crumbling before our eyes?

Michelle's persistence catches Julian off guard. She arrives at his apartment and forces him to change his rules for dealing with clients. At the same time as Michelle is breaking through Julian's veneer, the viability of his existence is questioned by the investigation into the rape and murder of Mrs. Rheiman. Without an alibi for the night of the murder, Julian finds that his clients have indeed turned on him and so too his retainers, who view his predicament as just deserts for his arrogance and disloyalty.

Slowly but surely, Julian's carefully constructed world is falling apart. The most dramatic rendering of this dismantling occurs when Julian ransacks his apartment in a desperate attempt to find evidence that has been planted to frame him for the crime. As Julian moves through the apartment, pulling books off the shelf and overturning furniture, the camera observes him from a shot at ceiling height. The angle of the lighting throws strips of shadow across the darkened room in a manner that recalls the lighting design used in *The Conformist*. As the camera slowly descends, the metallic drone on the soundtrack increases at pace with Julian's destruction of his apartment. Schrader's use of extreme angles echoes the schema used during the opening moments. It seems that the establishment of Julian's world and its destruction are part of the same impulse. Both moments have at their heart an anxiety about how far it is possible to fashion a sense of self and how easily this endeavor can fall apart.

In the wake of the destruction, the redemption of the protagonist only becomes possible when he accepts Michelle's love. Michelle sacrifices her reputation to provide Julian with an alibi, but in so doing she also frees herself from an unsatisfying marriage. The final scenes occur in nondescript police offices and in a prison visitors' room. The bright pastel colors that dominated the first half of the film are replaced by a series of washed-out blues and prison greys. The closing moments are also set off from what has come previously by the introduction of a series of slow fades between each scene. The final scene is another replay from *Pickpocket*: Julian leans his head against the glass separating him from Michelle's outstretched hand and states: "My God, Michelle, it's taken me so long to come to you."

How are we meant to read the film's shift in style and the personal transformation signaled by Julian's words? Clearly, Schrader wants to evoke the sense of a decisive action—but one very different from that found in the final moments of *Taxi Driver.* Whereas the overhead tracking shots away from the scene of Travis's crime seem determined to detach us from the protagonist, the closing moments of *American Gigolo* strive for something much closer to what Bresson achieved at the end of *Pickpocket.* "You are talking about a cold, cut-off person who has been denying his emotional and spiritual life, and in one bold moment everything breaks through and he makes physical contact with his true life, with the life of the heart and the soul" (Cousins). Schrader's description of the final moments of *Pickpocket* neatly sums up what is at stake in his own film: a transformation in the emotional and spiritual life of the protagonist. The difficult thing for the spectator is to reconcile this spiritual awakening with what has come before. "With *American Gigolo*," writes Nichols, "we expect resolution to come within Julian's everyday realm, the one in which we have been immersed. When it does not (due to the discrepant style of the ending), this points to the genuine impossibility of resolving the dilemma of Julian's self-contradictory nature within the context in which it arises because of the self-contradictory nature of that real, material context" (Nichols 12).

In *American Gigolo,* Schrader's dilemma is similar to the one he faced in *Hardcore*: how to do justice to a drama based on irreconcilable elements. In this case, Julian's desire to stand apart from emotional commitment is at odds with his belated acceptance of Michelle's love. Is it possible to keep these two things in mind without diminishing one or the other? Schrader's ability to fashion the style of the film around this dilemma was seen by a number of critics as a breakthrough. "What is notable about *American Gigolo,*" writes Combs, "is that Schrader's 'European' pretensions for the first time seem to have been integrated with the style of the film: the camera, here almost deliriously liberated from its prosaic functions in *Blue Collar* and *Hardcore,* drifts through the neighborhoods of Los Angeles and some rather splendid scenery on Julian's drive to Palm Springs in a way that almost out-Antonionis *Zabriskie Point* [1969]. The detachment for which the plot has to work so hard is quite gracefully achieved at this level" (Combs, Review of *American Gigolo* 88).

Changelings: *Cat People*

Detachment seems a strange word to use in the context of Schrader's early career, but it signals an important shift in the way he approached the telling of his stories. For Schrader, *American Gigolo* marked a significant advance in his confidence as a director: "I felt that I had arrived as a director; I felt confident about moving the camera and placing the camera. I *saw* the movie for the first time; I saw the whole notion of visual thinking that had first been suggested to me by [Charles] Eames—it now properly made sense to me" (*SOS* 166). Elsewhere, Schrader expands on the influence of the American designer, architect, and filmmaker: "Eames taught me that there is a visual logic in life and that to be a poet, or a poet of ideas . . . doesn't mean you have to use language" (*SOS* 26). As well as opening his eyes to the possibilities of images as ideas, Eames helped Schrader develop a conception of filmmaking as a practice of problem solving: "The common denominator of Eames's occupations is that he is, elementally, one thing: a problem-solver, with aesthetic and social considerations. He approaches life as a set of problems, each of which must be defined, delineated, abstracted, and solved. His architect's mind visualizes complex social patterns, twisting and folding like a three-dimensional blueprint. He respects the 'problem' not only as a means to an end but as an aesthetic pleasure in itself" (*SOS* 96).

When applied to filmmaking, this notion of problem solving means that each film takes its shape and form according to the problem or challenge in question. This does not preclude the idea of a directorial signature, but it does require the filmmaker to interpolate his own obsessions and interests across a range of different outcomes and forms. As Schrader explains in reference to the work of Stanley Kubrick: "There are different models for a film-maker, and the Hitchcock or Ford model is not necessarily the only one. I personally am more enamored of the Kubrick model, where one never knows what the next film is going to be like" (qtd. in Romney, "Following" 7). Schrader's adoption of a problem-solving approach means that it is difficult to maintain a consistent critical line on his films. His films take their lead from the problem at hand.

Although the idea for *American Gigolo* emerged out of a roundtable discussion during a class Schrader was teaching at UCLA, its central theme, concerning the inability to express love, had an immediate personal connection: "I came from a background in which physical contact was rare, and in my family was exacerbated to the point at which my father actually shook when he held you" (*SOS* 161). The script Schrader wrote directly after *American Gigolo,* "Born in the USA," later filmed as *Light of Day,* was also a personal project. When Schrader ran into difficulties raising finance for the script, he decided to change tack by agreeing to direct a film based on a script he had not written: "One of the reasons 'Born in the USA' was running into difficulties was that it was just too personal, so I said, 'OK, I'm going to do a genre film, a horror film, a special-effects film that will not be about me, and that will be a very salutary exercise'" (*SOS* 166).

Schrader has admitted that the other reason for taking on *Cat People* was to overcome an overwhelming sense of burnout as a writer. In one year, Schrader wrote five scripts: *Blue Collar, Hardcore, American Gigolo, Old Boyfriends,* and a never-produced Hank Williams biography. He spent the next three years directing three of these scripts. The only new writing during this period was his rewrite of the script of *Raging Bull.* Schrader's main contribution to this script was to introduce the character of Joey La Motta and to make the relationship between the two brothers, Joey and Jake, central to the drama. His other contribution was to foreground Jake's obsession with his "little girl's hands." Schrader describes how this obsession was incorporated in his unfilmed version of the prison scene: "Jake is in the cell and he's trying to masturbate and is unsuccessful, because every time he tries to conjure up an image of a woman he's known, he also remembers how badly he's treated her, so he's not able to maintain an erection. Finally he takes it out on his hands; he blames his hands and smashes them against the wall" (*SOS* 131).

Asked by Kevin Jackson why a number of his films—*The Yakuza, Rolling Thunder,* and *Taxi Driver*—contain scenes involving the mutilation of a hand or arm, Schrader cites a common self-destructive fantasy among writers: "It's like a painter fantasizing about blinding himself" (*SOS* 122). Viewed in the context of Schrader's own crisis as a writer, the exercising of this self-destructive fantasy in *Raging Bull* takes on a prescient quality: "I went to the typewriter and nothing, nothing came" (Dunne 86). Compounding Schrader's despair at this time was his grief over the death of his mother—an event powerfully dramatized some years later in *Light of Day.*

When the offer came from Universal to direct *Cat People,* Schrader heeded the advice of his agent and took on the project as a way of getting back to work. A couple of weeks into the shooting, his assumptions about the film changed dramatically: "I realized I *was* one of the characters. I was the John Heard character. . . . I realized that what I had here was an intellectual, older Travis Bickle. This is me and this is my Calvinistic notion of the postponement of pleasure and the kind of sanctity of sex where you can really only be in love with something better" (qtd. in Thomson 50–51). In his discussions with Jackson, Schrader describes how this transformation happened:

> Mainly in the way we evolved the character of the zookeeper played by John Heard as a sort of pursuer of a Beatrice figure. He's a man who lives with animals because he doesn't like humans very much. And then his Beatrice appears and his greatest fantasy has come true, because Beatrice is an animal. Well, as we developed the character he evolved more and more along the lines of myself, and then during the actual shooting of the film I became involved with Nastassia Kinski and became obsessed with her. So the story of the film started to become very personal, so much so that I wasn't really aware of how perverse it was getting. (*SOS* 166–67)

Schrader's insistence on identifying his own place within his films lends a special urgency to his treatment of themes concerning self-realization. This is evident in the struggles undergone by the protagonists in *Taxi Driver* and *American Gigolo*. It is also evident in the relationship between Irena Gallier (Nastassia Kinski) and Oliver Yates (John Heard) in *Cat People*. The premise for this relationship is drawn from Jacques Tourneur's earlier film of the same name. Rather than remaking Tourneur's film, Schrader updates the myth of an ancient race able to move between animal and human form by drawing out its darker sexual undertones. In terms of its visual design, *Cat People* continues the "high style" approach used in *American Gigolo*. In place of the cool pastels found in *American Gigolo*, *Cat People* employs a much richer pallet dominated by greens, oranges, and deep blues. The film shares with its predecessor a fondness for high-angle shots that crane down to track the movements of the characters in a manner that again reveals the influence of Bertolucci's camerawork in *The Conformist*. In *Cat People*, design, color, and staging all work to project a sense of the mythic onto the space around the characters.

In terms of its treatment of the characters' travails, *Cat People* offers an important recasting of those moments of individual transformation in *Taxi Driver* and *American Gigolo*. In *Taxi Driver*, Travis purifies his body in preparation for the mission that will validate his existence. In *American Gigolo*, Julian's transformation moves in the opposite direction to that of Travis: his carefully ordered existence is unraveled by the machinations of an unknown party that has turned against him. The changes in his circumstances presage a more profound transformation through love. In *Cat People*, transformation involves a physical metamorphosis of the most radical kind: from human to animal. The film literalizes the anxieties of dissolution that in the previous films were given a psychological rendering. People, animals, relations between brother and sister, and even the image itself have a strange uncertain quality. This is due to Scarfiotti's ornate production design and the lingering affect of Albert Whitlock's matte paintings that serve as backdrops in the prologue and elsewhere. The way these matte paintings fool the eye and beguile us with their artificial beauty sets the tone for the film's attempts to create a bridge between the images and symbols of night dreams and waking life.

"When I conceived *Cat People*," Schrader observes, "I decided to make a film about what [Jean] Cocteau called 'the sacred monsters,' the things that have galloped through man's dreams since time immemorial" (Dunne 88–90). *Cat People* lends these night creatures a daytime existence. Near the start of the film, a precisely staged dissolve substitutes a close-up of the eyes of a young tribal woman, who has just been initiated into the ways of her people, with a close-up of the eyes of Irena. She looks back at the camera with a slightly bewildered expression reminiscent of someone awaking from a dream. The camera follows her movements through the airport from a position just above the eye-line. After a few seconds, the camera descends, and we notice in the right-hand corner of the frame a figure in a dark suit obviously following Irena. This oddly threatening figure, we discover, is Paul (Malcolm McDowell), the brother Irena has not seen since they were separated as small children. Paul takes Irena back to the house he shares with a black housekeeper, Female (Ruby Dee). After dinner, he fills Irena in on some of the details concerning their parents' history. Later, as Irena is sleeping, Paul enters her room and leaps onto the foot of the bed frame, where he gazes at her sleeping form. We come to learn that Paul's strange behavior stems not from overeager sibling affection but from the fact that Irena is the only one with whom he is able to enter into a physical relationship without transforming into a leopard.

Irena's gradual realization of her condition coincides with the commencement of her amorous feelings for Oliver, a zoo curator struggling with his own frustrations and loneliness. The difficulties faced by Irena, Oliver, and Paul in achieving physical union highlight Schrader's interest in the original premise as a pretext for a story about the costs of sexual awakening. "It isn't a horror film, per se," Schrader explains, "though it uses the horror context to play upon our notions of sexuality, sexual presence, and sexual iconography" (qtd. in Rebello 40). We can get a better sense of the film's displacement of the horror genre by first considering the manifestation of horrific elements in *Taxi Driver*. In *Taxi Driver*, the world takes on the appearance of a horror film drawn directly from Travis's incipient psychosis, racism, and anxiety over sex. This anxiety manifests itself in his musings about pollution, bodily waste, and the city as "an open sewer." "Sometimes I can hardly take it," he tells Palantine. "Sometimes I go out and smell it, I get headaches it's so bad . . . I think that the president should just clean up this whole mess here, should just

Cat People: Paul (Malcolm McDowell) tries to convince Irena (Nastassia Kinski) of their secret lineage.

flush it right down the fucking toilet." The most resonate articulation of this anxiety is Travis's description of cleaning the come and blood off the backseat of the cab. Stern argues that, for Travis, blood and come are associated "because they both involve a spilling, a rupturing of the division between inside and outside, but also because they coalesce around the sexual" (Stern 55). This anxiety drives Travis to project his own sense of dirt and bodily waste onto others: "[H]e transforms his own semen into others' blood" (55).

In *Cat People,* the mixing of blood and semen is central to the film's depiction of sexual awakening. The day after Irena coyly confesses to Oliver's former lover and coworker, Alice Perrin (Annette O'Toole), that she is still a virgin, she witnesses one of the zoo employees lose his arm while trying to feed a caged leopard. The close-up of the blood splashing Irena's feet implicates her own sexual awakening with the violence of the leopard's actions. More than this, it makes the connection undeniable. Jonathan Romney observes that Schrader's literalization of the subtextual elements in the original version results in a very different type of drama:

"A film of absences is replaced by one of complete presence in which everything is there on the surface" (Romney, "New Ways" 149). For Romney, this results in a film constructed around a series of "rhetorical gestures" and allusions: "surface *'effects'* free of any visceral *effect*" (151). In fact, Schrader's film gives us something more contradictory. *Cat People* alludes to a set of preexisting narrative tropes and myths; but it also imbues these tropes and myths with a heightened sense of credulity. Indeed, the difficult thing about the film is not its element of self-consciousness but the extent to which Schrader plays it straight, evoking what he calls "a pre-*nouvelle vague* spirit, of those guys who did believe in magic—[Orson] Welles, [Georges] Franju, Cocteau, people who believed cinema was myth, before realism and didacticism took over" (Thomson 52).

Schrader's update of the original film is also distinguished by the way he merges the psychosexual dynamics of the central relationship with a concern for romantic love. As Schrader notes, Irena is Paul's Beatrice, the embodiment of romantic love in Dante Alighieri's *Vita Nuova*. Just

Cat People: Oliver (John Heard) awakens to
confront the black leopard.

before he first meets Irena, Oliver is working late in his office while listening to a tape of Dante's famous tale of romantic love. He stops the tape to recite the words, as if he is interpolating his own voice into Dante's narrative. In *Vita Nuova*, the narrator is so overwhelmed by his feelings for Beatrice that even the sight of his beloved throws his senses into a state of utter turmoil: "I come to see you hoping to be healed; / but if I raise my eyes to look at you / a trembling starts at once within my heart / and drives life out and stops my pulses' beat" (Alighieri 30). *Cat People* uses the fantastic possibilities of the horror film to literalize Dante's much older drama of love and bodily dissolution. In both works, love induces a physical as well as emotional transformation. Dante's narrator goes so far as to describe himself as love's "changeling" (26).

The dilemma faced by Irena, Oliver, and Paul also allows Schrader to restage one of his favorite Bressonian metaphors, the "two-faced prison": "[H]is characters are both escaping from a prison of one sort and surrendering to a prison of another. And the prison his protagonists ultimately escape is the most confining prison of all, the body" (Schrader, *Transcendental* 93). This metaphor encapsulates the ambivalent nature of self-realization in Bresson's work. In Schrader's films, self-realization comes at a price and only through a kind of self-mortification. This is why so many of the concluding moments of his films take place in literal prisons, for example, *American Gigolo, Patty Hearst,* and *Light Sleeper,* or else the prison is metaphorical, for example, the cab in *Taxi Driver.* In *Cat People* the prison is the zoo and its enclosures. Schrader departs from Bresson in his treatment of the body. In *Cat People,* the body is not only a prison but also something that must be awakened.

After her first sexual encounter with Oliver, Irena lies awake in bed. She gets up and walks to the bathroom. As she stands in front of the mirror, she reaches down with her hand and smears the blood from between her legs onto her mouth. Quickly washing the blood from her face and hands, she stares back at her troubled reflection and slowly steps away. When she returns to bed, Irena raises her hand in front of her face, as if checking the status of a thing that is a part of her yet also separate. Grounded in a recognizable disturbance of bodily sensation, Irena's actions prepare the audience for the more spectacular metamorphosis that occurs immediately after, when she changes from human form to a leopard.

Cat People: After her first sexual encounter with Oliver, Irena stares at her reflection in the mirror.

The consummation of the relationship releases Irena from the prison of her human form. The question then becomes: How will Oliver deal with this knowledge? As Andrew Sarris rightly notes in his review of the film, Oliver's refusal to relinquish his obsession for Irena is the key way Schrader subverts the content of the earlier film. In Schrader's retelling of the story, "[t]here are no longer any nonobsessive major characters. Oliver is in some ways crazier than Irena and Paul in his ultimate decision to love the woman in the panther as much as, if not even more than, he ever loved the panther in the woman" (Sarris 43). Oliver's obsession culminates when Irena returns and begs him to either kill her or grant her final release by making love to her one more time.

When the image fades back up, Oliver has returned to work as a curator. Since we last saw him, he has also reunited with Alice. We watch the reunited couple leave the offices together on their lunch break. But instead of immediately joining Alice, Oliver heads to the cages. Inside one of the cages, a black leopard paces back and forth. Oliver reaches through the bars and gives the leopard some food. Irena and Oliver have achieved freedom; both are now confined. The final shot of the film is a close-up of the leopard's eyes looking back at Oliver. In a standard ending for Schrader, the image freezes, and the words of the theme song by Moroder and David Bowie begin. It is interesting to consider why so many of Schrader's films—*Blue Collar, American Gigolo, Cat People, Mishima, Light of Day,* and *Light Sleeper*—end this way. Schrader's use of the freeze frame suggests something irreconcilable about the drama that has just concluded. It is not an ending to the story as such but a literal fixing in place of a dilemma—a final moment of fetishization and disavowal prior to the lights coming back on. At the end of *Cat People,* Oliver is back at work, and everyday life has resumed its course; but his obsession remains. As if to remind us of the ongoing nature of Oliver's predicament, just as we are about to rise from our seats, the frozen image snaps back to life, and the leopard releases one last growl that echoes across the closing credits.

The Lure of Biography:
Mishima: A Life in Four Chapters

Cat People illustrates how closely aligned issues of self-realization and self-dispersal are in Schrader's films. Finding oneself and losing oneself entirely are part of the same process by which one enters into contact with an other whose form changes before our eyes. "Because she was so young," Schrader notes about Kinski, the film's lead actress, "her face would literally change from day to day" (Thomson 52). For the director, also, each project is bound up with a task of self-realization. In *Cat People,* this involved beginning a personal relationship with the lead actress and the establishment of a connection with the central male character. Given this range of personal investments, it is not surprising that, on its release, *Cat People* was seen as an odd beast: not quite the horror film that fans of the genre were expecting, nor quite the Schrader film that critics and his supporters had come to expect: "Well, the horror audience went and said, 'Hey, this doesn't look like a horror film, it's not for us,' and the sophisticated audience went and said, 'Hey, this is just a horror film'" (*SOS* 172). Interestingly, Irena and Oliver are driven to consummate their relationship, despite their awareness of the consequences, by the agony of just such a half-realized transformation, of being neither one thing nor the other.

In the films that followed *Cat People,* the tension between authorial self-realization and the constraints of commercial filmmaking drew Schrader further away from large-budget, studio-financed filmmaking. He remained a Hollywood director; but, increasingly, his films came to represent a form of risk taking in an environment renowned for risk aversion. The most dramatic example of this conflicted relationship was his next film, *Mishima.* Filmed in Japan with a Japanese cast and a largely Japanese crew, the film inaugurated a break from the hothouse world of Hollywood filmmaking that was being pushed along by the success of blockbusters like *Raiders of the Lost Ark* (1981) and the first three films of the *Star Wars* series (1977–83). By taking on such a risky project at a time when many of his generation were heading in the opposite direction, Schrader was sending a clear message regarding his aspirations as a filmmaker. The production of *Mishima* also coincided with a period of significant change in the director's life. During his time in Japan, Schrader's partner and current wife, Mary Beth Hurt, gave birth to their first child. Perhaps more than anything else, this event tempered Schrader's identification with the destructive behavior of his protagonists.

During the production of *Mishima,* Schrader relied on two teams of bilingual speakers: one to communicate his directions to his Japanese cast, and the other to communicate with the crew. While this would have made filming difficult enough, Schrader also had to deal with an unusual challenge. Nearly half the film's budget, $2.5 million, was drawn from two Japanese investors: Fuji Television and Toho-Towa Distribution. The controversy surrounding Mishima's life was such that both investors refused to acknowledge their involvement in the project. The remaining $3.25 million of the film's budget came from Warners—largely due to the commercial clout of the film's executive producers, George Lucas and Francis Ford Coppola: "So while making the movie I had a very peculiar luxury, which was that of making a film that no one ever expected to make a dime. On the other hand, that entailed enormous pressure and responsibility, because there was no way you could turn round and say, 'Hey, look, I tried to make a buck, I failed, too bad.' The only criterion I could hold the film up to was that of excellence" (*SOS*

180). The outcome of this peculiar set of circumstances was Schrader's most formally ambitious film: "There's an element of perverse joy in it—just the fact that no one had done anything like that before and no one thought I could do it" (*SOS* 182).

Part of the challenge of *Mishima* involved making sense of the contradictory elements of Mishima's life and writings while dealing with the restrictions placed on the production by the writer's widow. *Mishima* stands as a turning point in Schrader's career not only because of the challenges faced in its production but also because it marks the end of one key thematic strand—Schrader's concern with suicidal glory initiated in *Taxi Driver*—and the beginning of an important new phase: Schrader's involvement in biographical filmmaking. During the 1980s, film biography became one of the hallmarks of Schrader's career. Combs links *Mishima* to *Patty Hearst* and the scripts for *The Last Temptation of Christ, Raging Bull,* and the unfilmed George Gershwin and Hank Williams biographies: "Given that *Mishima* is probably his most perverse and individualistic film to date, and *Patty Hearst* his most successful, biography does look like Schrader's métier." "His films," Combs adds, "are most alive when working their way into and then working their way out of a life, immersion and transcendence being the vital mechanism" (Combs, "Patty Hearst" 197). During the making of *Mishima,* Schrader explained his relationship to the story of the famous Japanese writer:

> I came to Mishima because his story is part of my fantasy world. . . . If I'm going to do a film about my own death-wishes, my own homo-erotic, narcissistic feelings, my own over-calculation of life and my own inability to *feel,* well, here's a man who has repeatedly stated those identical problems. I believe that this is the only way to do a biography which also has the force of a personal statement: two psyches have to be in sufficient synch to give you the liberty you need within the confines of what actually happened. (qtd. in Rayns 256)

Schrader's comments suggest that what is at stake in *Mishima* is not only the struggle to do justice to a life story based around various masks but also the struggle of the director to place himself within the film. Both struggles involve a displacement of biographical identity onto a question of form. In this sense, the film is deliberately speculative: "It does not propose to be the last word on Yukio Mishima; it just opens a lot of doors" (Jaehne, "Schrader's" 14). The way these doors are opened reveals much about Schrader's development as a filmmaker and the nature of biographical filmmaking.

Mishima is divided into four chapters: "Beauty," "Art," "Action," and "Harmony of Pen and Sword." Each chapter follows two distinct time frames: one concerns the unfolding of the events of November 25, 1970; the other charts key moments in Mishima's life leading up to this day. "Beauty" covers Mishima's preparations during the morning of the takeover of the army commander's offices. After completing the preparations and making a call to the press, Mishima leaves the house. The camera slowly zooms in on the author as he walks down the steps outside the house. But instead of following Mishima's movements away from the house, the camera continues to zoom toward a tiny figure in the background looking out the window. The film cuts to a shot inside the house. A small boy looks out the window. The scene onto which he gazes is no longer of Mishima's departure but a street. This shift in location, the switch to black and white, and the commencement of the first-person voiceover narration clarify that the small boy is Mishima

Mishima: Paul Schrader in front of a photograph of Ken Ogata as Yukio Mishima.

at the time when he lived with his ailing grandmother. It is Mishima's aristocratic and overly protective grandmother who introduces him to the theater. During one of these trips to the theater, Mishima witnesses something unexpected. As he rests with his grandmother in the foyer, the side door of a dressing room opens. Inside the dressing room, Mishima catches sight of an Onnagata—in traditional Japanese theater, the name given to a male performer specializing in female roles. The Onnagata turns to look at the inquisitive boy and languidly lifts a cigarette to his mouth. The unexpected appearance of the actor still in costume and the indolence of the gesture transfix the young author.

The second chapter, "Art," also hinges on an exchange of glances. This chapter returns to the day of the takeover. Mishima and his acolytes are traveling to the army headquarters. During the journey, Mishima catches sight of himself in a poster decorating the window of a bookstore. This encounter triggers the recommencement of the main biographical component dealing with the rise of Mishima's renown as a writer in postwar Japan, a time when he turned his attention to shaping not only words and stories but also the physical form of his body. Mishima's voiceover explains his motivation: "Creating a beautiful work of art and becoming beautiful oneself are identical." Later, Mishima expands on the implications of this statement: "[A] man's determination to become beautiful is always a desire for death." The third chapter, "Action," covers the formation of the Shield Society and Mishima's confrontation with striking student radicals at Tokyo University. Mishima's failure to convince the students of his views on Japanese society is echoed in the final chapter, "Harmony of Pen and Sword," in which Mishima and his collaborators arrive at the garrison headquarters. After barricading themselves inside the commander's office, they force him to assemble the garrison. With media helicopters flying overhead, Mishima stands on the balcony outside the office lecturing the assembled soldiers. Drowned out by the soldiers' jeers, Mishima retreats into the office where he prepares to commit *seppuku*.

The division of the film into four chapters detailing the events of November 25 and jumping back to cover formative incidents in the author's life is complicated further by the inclusion of three highly theatrical dramatizations of scenes from Mishima's writings.[6] The choice and placement of these dramatizations parallel events occurring in Mishima's

Mishima: The young Mishima (Masato Aizawa) transfixed by the image of the martyrdom of Saint Sebastian. In 1961, Mishima re-created this image in *Ordeal by Roses,* a book of photographic portraits produced with the Japanese photographer Eikoh Hosoe.

life. *Temple of the Golden Pavilion* draws its inspiration from Mishima's childhood frailties. It deals with the frustrations of a young temple acolyte, Mizoguchi (Yasosuke Bando), struggling with his own physical inhibitions and the beauty of the Golden Pavilion. *Kyoko's House* is about a narcissistic young actor, Osamu (Kenji Sawada), and his increasingly masochistic relationship to Kiyomi (Reisen Lee)—an older woman to whom his own mother is in financial debt. In exchange for canceling the debt, Kiyomi forces Osamu to pledge his own body. *Runaway Horses* echoes the final phase of Mishima's life. It concerns a young cadet, Isao (Toshiyuki Nagashima), who forms a secret cell dedicated to returning Japan to its former glories. The cell plans to assassinate politicians and industrialists viewed as responsible for the corrupt state of modern Japanese society. After the activities of the cell are discovered, Isao is imprisoned. He escapes from jail and murders a businessman. He is last seen arriving at a beach where he prepares to commit *seppuku*.

In each of the three storylines, the final climatic moment—Mizoguchi burning down the Golden Temple; the death of Osamu; Isao's *seppuku*— is held back until the end of the film. During the closing moments, the film returns to the drama unfolding at the garrison headquarters. As Mishima plunges the knife into his body, the three dramatizations and the biographical details of Mishima's life story culminate in an act of willed self-destruction.

Schrader creates a sense of the contradictions in Mishima's life, the central themes of his art, and the interplay between these realms through the elaborate intertwining of biographical elements and fictional stagings. This method also allows Schrader to solve another more directly cinematic dilemma: how to distance *Mishima* from traditional approaches to film biography. The biopic continues to be one of the staple genres of feature-film production, undergoing a number of different mutations and shifts in emphasis over time. As George F. Custen points out: "[T]he definition of what constitutes a bio-pic—and with it, what counts as fame—shifts anew with each generation. . . . It is not that each generation creates or discovers necessarily new forums for fame; rather, certain careers and types of people become the prime focus of public curiosity in each generation" (Custen 6–7). Schrader's interest in Mishima's life story was based on the writer's exemplification of impulses and feelings that were part of Schrader's own psychology.

The other reason concerns the relationship between writing and life: "[T]he great dilemma [Mishima] faced was a Western dilemma too: for the modern writer, when does life supersede writing, when are words insufficient? He was the first man really to formulate a problem which has been bedevilling writers ever since the advent of television, which is that writers are now a lot better known as performers in the media than for their writing" (SOS 173).

Mishima's desire to transcend the powerlessness of words by turning his own life into an act of creation poses a problem for traditional biographical approaches based on the uncovering of a fundamental truth. For Schrader, this dilemma is linked to a more general problem with film biography. "I have problems with conventional biographical films; I just can't bear to see movies about real events that falsify them. . . . I've more or less decided to stay away from biography in future because I find that I always impose these structures so that I don't have to fabricate events—the fabrication occurs in the structure rather than in the episodes" (SOS 127). As Schrader notes, all films about real people have at their core an elaborate act of fabrication. It is not that film biography

Mishima: Mishima (Ken Ogata) performing the role of ancient samurai. This pose also appears in *Ordeal by Roses*.

is any more fictional than other styles of film. Rather, the historical existence of the person renders the artifice of representation more overt. The knowledge of this existence gets in the way of the pleasure we take in knowing that something is false *and* the ability to suspend this knowledge of falsehood.

Schrader's response to this problem is common to other, more overtly modernist filmmakers: he changes the premise of the game. Rather than disguising the fabrication, he makes it even more visible. In *Mishima* this heightening of artifice is achieved through the film's elaborate narrative structure—its switches between different time frames, the inclusion of dramatizations of portions from three of Mishima's novels—and its self-conscious approach to design. Ishioka Eiko's design of the three segments drawn from Mishima's novels—using minimal sets and rich artificial colors to designate areas of action—distinguishes these segments from the naturalism of the biographical sections designed by Takenaka Kazuo, a veteran of Japan's Toho Studios. "When you see Eiko's sets," Schrader notes, "there's nothing of Takenaka in them, and there's nothing of her in his sets either" (qtd. in Rayns 259). The self-conscious approach to design frees the filmmaker from the lie of biography. Paradoxically, it also allows him to capture something central to Mishima's life: not only the distance between art and the thing it approximates but also the desire to overcome this distance through an act of self-creation.

Instead of simply telling the story of Mishima's life, Schrader's film approximates a form that embodies its contradictions. The relationship between the film and its subject is not simply imitative but also performative: it is defined by an explicit exchange between the body of the film and the body it seeks to represent. In traditional film biography, this exchange is usually disguised or located outside of the film proper. In *Mishima,* Schrader draws attention to its operation by making it the instigator for other exchanges. At times, these exchanges are overt—for example, the moment near the start of the film when the camera's attention passes from the adult Mishima leaving the house to his childhood representative looking on in the background; or when a head-and-shoulder shot of Mishima as a stuttering schoolboy overlaps with a shot of a similarly afflicted Mizoguchi from *Temple of the Golden Pavilion.* At other times, the exchange is more implicit, as when Mishima catches sight of the Onnagata in his dressing room. The prolonged con-

Mishima: The set designed by Ishioka Eiko for *Temple of the Golden Pavilion*. In this image, Mizoguchi (Yasosuke Bando) watches as his disabled friend Mariko (Hisako Manda) tries to elicit the sympathy of passing women.

tact between the small boy and the actor suggests the stirrings of the young author's sexual impulses and a type of temporal overlap whereby different Mishimas seem to coexist.

Regardless of their different styles, in each instance the moment of exchange enacts a type of formal disturbance whereby, for a brief moment, past and present are unsettled. This reconfiguring of the scene keeps the narrative from congealing, but it also allows something to become visible that would otherwise remain hidden. This thing made visible is a way of responding to a subject that is at once flesh and blood and filmic, a subject divided across different contexts (past and present, biographical and fictional) and moments of self-regard. Through the creation of such a complex relation, Schrader opens biographical fiction to different kinds of narrative configurations in which the historical body instigating the drama is no longer pushed to one side but made to count and given a performative presence. Does all this make Schrader a modernist filmmaker? Or is it the case of a problem solver endeavoring to do justice to the stories at hand? Rather than answering this question, the films that followed *Mishima* make it even harder to come up with a definitive response.

The Catastrophe of Identity: *Light of Day* and *Patty Hearst*

For a number of critics, *Mishima* confirmed the extent to which Schrader aligns his own story with that of his troubled protagonists. "The contradictions and confusions of the director's past," wrote Combs, "have here become embodied in his protagonist, even down to the dubious emotional effect of defining the author through his fictions" (Combs, Review of *Mishima* 301). And, certainly, the director's own pronouncements on the appeal of the film's central character add weight to such a reading. These statements overlook the fact that, during the 1980s, the project that had the most direct personal significance for Schrader was not *Mishima* but a more low-key autobiographical drama "about unflashy people who live unflashy lives" (*SOS* 188). As mentioned earlier, Schrader had tried unsuccessfully to secure funding for "Born in the USA" immediately after *American Gigolo*. Determined to get the film made, he returned to the project after completing *Mishima*. In the interim, Schrader changed a key aspect of the script by replacing the relationship between the two brothers with one involving a brother and sister. The other change was to replace the original title, which had been adopted by Bruce Springsteen for his hugely popular album, with *Light of Day*.[7]

By taking as its inspiration Schrader's relationship to his mother, *Light of Day* bookends the story begun in *Hardcore*. Schrader describes the film's emotional climax, where Patti Rasnick (Joan Jett) reconciles with her dying mother (Gena Rowlands), as "more or less word for word what I went through with my mother" (*SOS* 185). Although the focus of the film is split between Patti and her brother, Joe (Michael J. Fox), the driving force is clearly Patti. Patti's combative relationship with her mother provides the central dramatic conflict. Whereas the mother draws strength from her religious beliefs, Patti finds strength in playing music. Apart from her small son, Benji (Billy Sullivan), Patti's sole focus is the Barbusters, a part-time rock-and-roll band in which Joe also plays. More than just something to fit in around other commitments, the Barbusters is Patti's way of escaping the claustrophobia and inertia of her surroundings.

Patti's rebellious behavior exemplifies an impulse also evident in the coked-out desperation of the three friends in *Blue Collar* and Kristen's flight in *Hardcore*. For Schrader, this impulse is summed up by The Animals' song, "We've Gotta Get Out of This Place" (*SOS* 148). It is an impulse that was part of his own upbringing in Grand Rapids and one that he keeps coming back to in his films. In *Light of Day*, the spokesperson for this feeling is Patti: she is the one who provides the band with direction and the one who most clearly refuses to live her life according to the rules set by the community. In contrast, Joe seems content to occupy his time covering for Patti's misdemeanors and playing the role of surrogate father for Benji. Despite his levelheaded approach to things, Joe also shows signs of the self-defeating behavior that we have learned to recognize from other characters. His string of poorly chosen dates suggests a quieter variation of the self-imposed loneliness that Schrader first pursued in *Taxi Driver*. In fact, the song that Joe and Benji improvise—"You Got No Place to Go"—could serve as the mantra for a number of Schrader's incapacitated male characters that find their social worlds reduced to a few small rooms. But whereas in other films Schrader grants these characters a degree of escape—no matter how contradictory or ambivalent—in *Light of Day* there seems to be no way out of the claustrophobia and inertia.

At the end of the film, Patti and the Barbusters are performing in front of much the same drunken crowd that was listening to the band earlier in the film. *Light of Day* is about dreams that don't go anywhere and everyday realities that get in the way of grand aspirations. The film counters these bleak undercurrents by emphasizing the sheer pleasure derived from playing music. "[O]ne of the things I was trying to get across in *Light of Day*," Schrader observes, "was rock and roll's function in everyday life. So many rock-and-roll movies revolve around the Cinderella myth of fame and wealth and girls, and what is missed in all those films is that rock and roll has a day-to-day practical function in the lives of thousands of people and thousands of little bands in thousands of little cities all over the world. . . . They may have dreams of glory, but what it's really about is release" (*SOS* 185).

Alongside this concern with the place of music in everyday life is something less obvious on first viewing: a concern with the importance of belief—whether it be the mother's religious belief or Patti's belief in music. "I've been trying to live my life by an idea," Patti tells Joe. "Rock and roll! That's an idea!" These words echo those of Joe's father (Jason Miller) when he tries to explain the sort of life he has made with his wife: "She gave me faith. What else is there?" Despite the father's shrunken stature, there is nothing patronizing or trite about this statement, nothing that would lead us to question its validity. "What else is there?" is the question that Patti throws back at Joe when he tries to get her to explain her behavior. The sense of symmetry between mother and daughter is reaffirmed in the film's closing stages when Patti returns to help nurse her mother during the final days of her illness. In their last encounter, Patti reveals to her mother the secret of Benji's paternity, and the mother confesses to Patti that she was always the one she loved the most. Faith in God and faith in music, mother and daughter: while not exactly two sides of the same coin, these characters are indeed kindred spirits. They embody the sense of push-pull that is central to the struggle for identity in *Light of Day*.

Light of Day: Paul Schrader discusses a scene with Joan Jett, who plays Patti. Seated next to Jett is Michael J. Fox, who plays her brother, Joe.

Despite the highly personal nature of the story, Schrader regards *Light of Day* as a failure. His frustrations have to do with the casting of the two lead roles and the film's lack of a distinct visual style. As Schrader has admitted, his disappointment also stems from the fact that *Light of Day* was too personal. In basing the film on his relationship with his mother, Schrader was unable to achieve the distance necessary to escape the claustrophobia of the film's working-class setting. "I would never again make a film with that kind of meat-and-potatoes style. I mean, there are scenes in a film that you would shoot in a meat-and-potatoes style because it's the only real way to do that scene, but I would never conceive of another film with the approach I used on *Light of Day*" (*SOS* 188).

In his next film, Schrader once again changes tack by adopting a perspective and visual style very different from that of *Light of Day*. In an analysis of *Patty Hearst*'s place in Schrader's body of work, Combs notes that, on first glance, the story of Patty Hearst's capture by the Symbionese Liberation Army (SLA), her fifty-seven days of confinement in a closet, and her induction into the SLA and eventual recapture and imprisonment by the FBI "looks exactly the opposite of the kind of self-dramatising life that [Schrader] needs" (Combs, "Patty Hearst" 197). *Patty Hearst* takes its place in Schrader's body of work because it is a story about the violent and often contradictory ways in which the self is formed and broken down. And as in *American Gigolo, Taxi Driver,* and *Light of Day,* this process is never simply one of self-fashioning; it is also implicated in a set of complex interpersonal relationships. As Combs perceptively recognizes, the inference raised by the film's depiction of Patty's ordeal is that the self is always capable of being "made something not its own."

At the start of the film, an elevated crane shot tracks Patty (Natasha Richardson) walking through a crowd of students at the University of California at Berkeley. Momentarily lost within the crowd, she reemerges just as the camera descends. The voiceover is taken from Patty Hearst's autobiography:

> I enjoyed a normal childhood. My four sisters and I weren't raised like rich kids. We were privileged, even overprivileged . . . not spoiled. I knew best what was right and wrong for me. Most things came easily

. . . sports, social relationships, schoolwork, life. I grew up in a sheltered environment, supremely self-confident. I knew, or I thought I knew, who I was. . . . More a doer than a thinker, an athlete than a student, a social being than a loner. . . . I was ever practical. I could see people in situations plainly, without frills. I never doubted my ability to handle myself well in any circumstance. . . . Of course, there is little one can do to prepare for the unknown.

As the final sentence is uttered, Patty turns and faces the camera. A split second later, the image freezes. From this point on, all of Patty's assertions about her self and her capacities are dismantled: her ordeal is to become strange to herself. This becoming strange is suggested by the freeze frame—usually a marker of a film's end rather than its beginning. It is also suggested by the look of bewilderment and apprehension on her face. It is as if the ordeal to come has already left its mark on the past—or at least the film's ability to reflect on this past. This sense of the future's imprint on the past is also evident in the sequence of family photographs taken from the Hearst family album that serves as background for the opening credits. The sense of normality that we might associate with images of birthday parties and family picnics is discolored by the looping of Patty's voice on the soundtrack: "Mom, Dad? . . . Who are you?" At this stage, it is not clear as to whom this question is directed. Patty's parents? Herself? Or perhaps the unknown that one cannot prepare for?

Schrader's reasons for agreeing to direct Nicholas Kazan's adaptation of Hearst's autobiography, *Every Secret Thing*, relate to his disappointment over the failure of *Light of Day*: "There was a purely pragmatic reason for making the film, which was that the depression brought about by the failure of *Light of Day* was rather crushing, because it was both a personal failure and a career failure. So I was very anxious to get back in the saddle, and this was a film that they would green light just as soon as a director said 'Yes'" (*SOS* 193). By agreeing to direct the film for a low fee and a small budget ("just under $4 million"), Schrader was also able to push the film in directions not possible with a more expensive project (Jaehne, "Patty" 26). Schrader attributes the film's lack of commercial success to poor decision making by the distributor. But he also concedes that the real reason for the film's commercial failure may lie with its presentation of the protagonist.

Especially during the first thirty minutes of the film, when she is abducted and locked in the closet by her captors, Patty functions as a voice curiously detached from its body, commenting on the action from a position somewhere above the huddled mass on the closet floor. Patty's passivity presented the greatest challenge for filmmaker and audience: "The definitive problem with *Patty Hearst*—and this is the reason that other directors turned the project down—is that it deals with a passive protagonist. Movies are about people who *do* things. The number one fantasy of the cinema is that we can do something—we are relatively impotent in our own lives so we go to movies to watch people who are in control of their lives. *Patty Hearst* violates the cardinal rule of cinema" (*SOS* 189).

Schrader's response to the problem of Patty's passivity was to energize the space around her, thus conveying to the audience the nature of her ordeal without reducing Patty to the status of victim. During the first half-hour of the film, each time the door of Patty's closet is opened, the expressionistic high-contrast lighting and the low camera angles present her abductors as faceless figures emerging from deep within a recurring nightmare. Even more disturbing than these visions from the closet floor are a series of high-angle shots of the activities occurring outside the closet; the camera descends into the darkened rooms as if it were descending into a pit. It is as if Patty's worst fear of being buried alive is continually replayed for audience and captive to share. Only when Patty is let out of the closet and her blindfold is removed does the dread start to lift, and the style of the film becomes less assaultive.

If Patty represents the spectacle of an identity in free fall, the representation of her captors offers no firm counterpoint. During the opening part of the film, the members of the SLA are presented as two-dimensional silhouettes framed in the doorway of Patty's closet. There is literally no substance to these silhouetted figures—just shapes and voices spouting revolutionary slogans and invective. Eventually, Patty is allowed to move out of her closet. We see her being bathed by one of her female captors and asked about her sexual feelings by another. These are the first steps in the transformation of her relationship with the SLA from captive to collaborator.

The relationship between Patty and the SLA is underpinned by a deeper complicity apparent from the start. Both Patty and the SLA share a problem common to a number of Schrader's central characters: self-realization. For both, the only way to achieve this is through an engagement with the rituals of theater. To convince the SLA of her commitment to the revolutionary struggle, Patty has to learn her lines and join in the rehearsals and training routines. The consequences of blowing her lines are simple. As Cinque (Ving Rhames) explains just before they enter the bank: "Fuck it up—you're dead." For the members of the SLA, the inherently performative nature of their struggle for self-realization is even more overt. The most comic example of this occurs when one member of the group, Teko (William Forsythe), paints his face black and practices his jive talk in front of a mirror. On a more general level, everything the SLA does is carried out with an eye to how it will be received by its primary audience, the media. After inducting Patty into the cell, Cinque exclaims: "What a propaganda coup. . . . Time for a photo session."

Patty Hearst: The robbery of a branch of the Hibernia Bank in San Francisco with SLA members: Fahizah (Olivia Barash), Cinque (Ving Rhames), and Patty, a.k.a. Tania (Natasha Richardson).

The historian Nancy Isenberg points out that the SLA's brand of revolutionary activism has close connections to forms of 1960s political theater, such as happenings and guerrilla theater, that were highly conscious of the role of the media and the imbrication of the political and the performative in everyday life (Isenberg 641). The constant training, preparation, and rehearsal that took up so much of the SLA's time bind their existence to a context of theatrical activism that was very much part of the historical moment. But these activities also suggest a close connection to a model of obsession found in earlier characters such as Travis, Julian, and Mishima. The ritualized actions of these characters give rise to a type of performative realization whose pleasures are "in the processes *before* action of stealthily watching, planning and staging" (Martin, *"Fingers"* 15). Collectively, the members of the SLA reproduce this model of obsession. Their focus is on the beauty of their words and purity of a pursuit untainted by any engagement with the world outside the terms they have established. This is why the world outside the safe house is strangely redundant. It is only allowed to filter in through newspaper headlines and TV and radio reports—intermittent shafts of outside influence much like the light that creeps in under the drawn curtains.

Even when the safe house burns down in a firefight with the Los Angeles police, and Patty is forced to take to the road with Teko and Yolanda (Frances Fisher), there is no letup from this tightly bound existence. The only difference is that the death of Cinque and others in the firefight gives Patty's rambling thoughts more space, more opportunity to take center stage. But these thoughts voice a state of waiting, watching, and preparing for something else to come along and take over: "For days, I'm in a world of my own, talk to no one, not a word. . . . I go deeper and deeper inside myself. . . . I read, smoke, try to keep out of the way." This period of interregnum is brought to a halt when the FBI storms the safe house. Schrader marks this moment's connection to Patty's earlier abduction by the SLA by replaying the shot of an exploding light bulb, thus suggesting the end of one type of imprisonment and the commencement of a new one.

The Paradox of Acting

In the final section of the film, dealing with the events following Patty's recapture, Schrader uses the device of establishing a clearly defined stage space to present a strategy meeting by prosecuting attorneys. The meeting takes place in a room without a ceiling. Initially located outside the room, the camera rises and then descends to circle the prosecutors. Schrader explains the connection between the use of this type of staging in *Mishima* and its reappearance in *Patty Hearst:*

> The reason I did it in *Mishima* was that I wanted to create a sense of the author's eye and of these events existing in limbo. Those little glowing rooms simulate the writer's vision. In *Patty Hearst* there is only one scene in which she is not a participant; every other scene is from her point of view. But it's important at some stage to get a sense of how the outside world viewed her, so I struck upon the idea of using the little glowing room again, where all these men—importantly, men—are walking around determining her fate. (*SOS* 196)

The artificiality of the glowing room allows the film to break from the point of view of the central subject. The implementation of a representational style distinct from what comes before signals this break. But if we push the effects of this break a little further, other consequences arise that relate directly to the agendas driving the biopic. As suggested earlier in relation to *Mishima,* the appearance of the glowing room functions as a moment of formal disturbance. It marks a shift to a presentational style of filming that highlights the film's own processes—hence the importance of Schrader's decision to commence so many of these scenes from a shot that reveals not only the glowing room but the darkened spaces that surround it. Like the darkened spaces outside Patty's closet that are full of menace, these spaces have an affective force: they register everything about the story that can't be explained or must be left out for the story to take place. As the mark of a necessary exclusion, they remind us that the film represents a necessarily incomplete account. Once such darkened spaces are acknowledged, they start to appear everywhere. As suggested by Patty's look of bewilderment and apprehension in the pre-credit sequence, they even have a retrospective force, clouding not only one's vision of the present but also one's ability to reflect on the past.

Commenting on the implications of Schrader's approach to the telling of Patty's story, Duncan Webster argues that the film's play of styles refuses to endorse a single account of the ordeal: "It would seem, and I think this is the lesson of Patty Hearst for the analysis of popular narratives, or journalism, photography and the media, that the 'real story' is the generation of versions of that story" (Webster 20). Isenberg also connects the cultural significance of Patty's ordeal to a larger dilemma concerning authoritative meaning: "[Patty's] story at once registers and resists the desire to find a single meaning. Despite all attempts by journalists, psychiatrists, and jurists to explain her persona through either the tragic story of a female captive/brainwashed victim or the dark comedy of the spoiled rich girl/pseudo revolutionary, her gendered identity cannot be fixed. . . . An authentic Hearst was a hard identity to find either before or during the trial. The courtroom drama also failed to unveil an original script" (Isenberg 640–41, 647).

In Schrader's depiction of the trial, the prosecuting attorney (John Achorn) tests Patty's defense by asking: "[T]o a large degree you were acting, were you not?" She replies: "Yes." The prosecutor presses further: "Are you a good actress, would you say? . . . Are you acting now?" For Patty and the film, these are impossible questions to answer because they require a position of authority on the story being told. Traditionally, film biography secures such a position through the inclusion of scenes or dramatic devices such as voiceover that clarify the circumstances and motivations driving the central character's actions. Patty's voiceover serves a different purpose: "I say nothing. I'm happy to have headaches. Happy to be constipated. Happy to be accepted rather than killed." Instead of clarifying the significance of her behavior—helping us to ascertain whether she is acting or not—Patty's voiceover catalogs her physical and emotional subjection: "I sleep all the time. I have no strength. I couldn't stand even if I were free to walk away. . . . My body's giving up."[8]

Combs identifies this emphasis on the presentation of states of being rather than uncovering internal motivations as a defining feature of Schrader's work: "Schrader gives us the mask of the thing, not the thing itself. There's often a baffled quality to his films, which drive their characters to a crisis of faith or identity, but then treat it in terms of a rather schematic, studiously blocked and timed action scenario" (Combs, "Patty Hearst" 200). Combs returns to the importance of the mask for Schrader: "[F]or a film-maker preoccupied with inner struggle, he deals remarkably little in psychology. It is back to masks again, and there is no way, and perhaps no need, to explain them" (200). According to Combs, the investment in masks becomes a self-enclosure that neither the characters nor the films can escape. While there is no escape from masks in Schrader's films, this does not necessarily lead, as Combs claims, to the relative safety of action scenarios. As illustrated by *Mishima* and *Patty Hearst*, Schrader's films establish forms of biographical storytelling that mark identity as a problem, as something without stable essence and thus only known through its various performative engagements. This is why, when Schrader is asked whether or not Patty was acting, his answer is deliberately ambivalent: "It's a mystery, a genuine conundrum, and I had to realize that the answer to it was "yes" and "no" all the time" (qtd. in Combs, "Patty Hearst" 198).

As presented by Schrader, Patty is and isn't acting—at the same time. Patty's story is doubly theatrical: it occurs within a scenic space defined by expressionistic set pieces (such as the representations of the safe houses as darkened pits, the strategy meeting by prosecuting attorneys, and a montage of psychiatrists throwing questions at Patty and pronouncing on her ordeal) while at the same time calling to mind the Paradox of Acting identified by Denis Diderot in the eighteenth century. According to Diderot, the great actor is someone who has mastered the technique of imitating emotions yet feels nothing. "If the great actor were full, really full, of feeling," Diderot asks, "how could he play the same part twice running with the same spirit and success?" (Diderot 14). Because of his or her special capacity to simulate, the great actor undermines the belief that we can distinguish between being and acting. Schrader's claim that Patty was and wasn't acting does something similar. It suggests an identity unable to be separated from the roles and performances it takes on. The film makes explicit what Diderot's paradox implicitly affirms: identity is most properly manifested through its simulation. This ambivalent realization underpins the conventions structuring the biopic: we recognize the identity of the person through the performance in front of us.

Jean-Louis Comolli recasts Diderot's paradox from the point of view of the spectator: "[I]t is him and it is not, always and at the same time; we believe in it and we do not, at the same time. Neither of the terms ever really prevails over the other, each keeps the other as a ground against which it stands out, each bounces off the trampoline of the other" (Comolli 48). *Patty Hearst* and *Mishima* add another layer to this scenario by exploring what happens when the historical person is only known as a conundrum of different media images and performances. What status does the film have in relation to the "original" it attempts to represent? We are back at the issue of a performative rather than mimetic mode of representation in which claims to truth are abjured in favor of a system of exchange that links the film to the historical subject it seeks to represent. In this system of exchange, no one figure has authority. Each is acting and being at the same time. And just as there is no original script, there is no original performance by which to judge all the other performances. Each performance brings Patty and Mishima into being yet removes them from themselves.

Strangers to Ourselves: *Auto Focus*

The final scene of *Patty Hearst* occurs in prison sometime after Patty has been found guilty. She is discussing her predicament with her father (Ermal Williamson). For most of the scene, she is presented in medium close-up talking to her father, who is positioned on the other side of the table and just to the left of the camera. Patty wants to replace her lawyer and wage a public campaign to prove her innocence: "I hope to let people see the real me. To demystify myself." The version of Patty Hearst represented in this scene is quite different from the ones we have previously seen. No longer willing to remain passive, she appears determined to take control of her situation. Interestingly, when the film was shown to Patty Hearst, to Schrader's surprise, this was the scene that caused a problem:

> You know it's her moment; we've been telling the story from a couple different points of view for 90 minutes. Now it's her turn. This is her moment, so I just put her in front of the camera and let her have her say. . . . All that stuff where she's abused and put upon, that was okay. . . .

But when she is shown standing up for herself, she claimed she looked cold: "I look calculating. I look like a bitch. You can't have that." But then that's the only person in the movie that approximates who she is now. (qtd. in Jaehne, "Patty" 26)

At the end of the scene, Patty's resolve to change the public's perception of her culminates in a bold statement of defiance: "Pardon my French, Dad, but . . . fuck 'em . . . fuck them all." This statement can be read as an expression of Patty's refusal to accede to the views of others. Viewed in the context of her previous experiences, however, "fuck them all" has a quite different set of associations. It suggests something irreconcilable about the "real me" that Patty wishes to convey to the public. "Fuck them all" carries with it the echo of those voices Patty was forced to listen to as she lay on the closet floor. It indicates how thoroughly these voices have become Patty's own voice, a voice marked by an experience of becoming strange to itself.

While they may project their sense of estrangement onto others, their own internal discord haunts Schrader's characters. In *Taxi Driver,* Scorsese provides the perfect endnote for the central character's estrangement when he speeds up Travis's startled response to his own reflection in the rearview mirror. In *Cat People,* Irena stares long and hard at her reflection in the bathroom mirror. Does this image belong to me? Or is it the property of another? In *Auto Focus,* the object at which Bob Crane stares is not a mirror but a television screen that plays back his various sexual exploits recorded on early-version videotape. While Crane's moments of self-regard are not marked by the same sense of inner turmoil found in *Taxi Driver* or *Cat People,* they are just as disturbing in their depiction of a male identity hopelessly dispersed across different contexts and performances.

Schrader links the life story of Crane to that of other characters: "This is a character not unlike characters I've done before, who have a disconnect in their lives, who want one thing but do another, see themselves as one thing but behave in a counter-productive way. And out of that disconnectedness comes an obsession, whether it is homicidal, or a conspiracy theory as in *Affliction.* Bob Crane had this very fundamental disconnectedness, which is that he saw himself as a very likeable, normal, one-woman, family kind of guy, but behaved in another fashion" (*SOS*

266). As depicted by Schrader, Crane's philandering, his passion for group sex and swinger's parties coordinated by his friend John Carpenter (Willem Dafoe), are not in and of themselves the problem. The problem is Crane's blithe refusal to recognize that his private behavior is at odds with his public persona as an affable television star made famous through the role of Colonel Hogan on "Hogan's Heroes." This lack of introspection singles Crane out from other characters. But it also presented the filmmaker with a challenge: "[H]ow do you do a film about a superficial man without making a superficial film?" (*SOS* 266).

Schrader's answer was to present Crane's predicament through the prism of his environment. In this film, the environment rather than the consciousness of the central character registers the most dramatic change. Schrader attributes this device to the film's production designer, James Chinlund: "[H]e thought that, as the movie went along, there should be an accretion of clutter: moving from the clean 1950s all-American house to the jumble of video-cables in the 1970s" (*SOS* 268). Schrader's inspiration was to apply this shift in design to the whole film: "film-stock, color saturation, camera work, make-up, hair, wardrobe, music. It all slowly degrades" (268). By the end of the film, the hand-held camera, distorted music, and overexposed backgrounds register a strong sense of a life ill at ease. It is as if the movie has shed its skin and become something darker.

For someone whose external circumstances change so dramatically, it is striking how little Crane's manner changes. The Bob Crane who attends church with his family at the start of the film is the same Bob Crane who performs for the TV cameras on the set of "Hogan's Heroes" or who waves to the video camera as he is fucking a woman from behind. Even when they are staring him in the face, Crane is either unwilling or incapable of registering the consequences of his actions. This dissociation comes to the fore when Crane and Carpenter are viewing one of their recordings of a group-sex encounter. As he watches the tape, Crane spots a dark object on his ass. After pausing and rewinding the tape, Crane discovers, to his horror, that the object is Carpenter's hand. Despite Carpenter's explanation that this is the sort of thing that happens during an orgy, Crane calls him a "fucking pervert . . . a fegollah" and storms out of the apartment, vowing never to return. Crane's refusal to accept Carpenter's groping hand is clearly the expression of a fundamental hy-

Auto Focus: John Carpenter (Willem Dafoe) draws
Bob Crane's (Greg Kinnear) attention to some of
the finer points of their homemade video porn.

pocrisy. It is also the mark of a strange form of detached consciousness
that is able to separate itself from the scene in which it is immersed.

Near the end of the film, Carpenter drops by Crane's house to show
him his latest gadget: a timer that will allow them to tape shows off the
TV. As Carpenter explains: "If you want to watch Johnny Carson at
11:30, and we're out hunting chicks, we set the timer. Boom! We watch
it in the morning." Although Crane is clearly impressed, problems with
his home life have left him glum. He begins to tell Carpenter about his
problems, but his attention is distracted by the moaning sounds ema-
nating from the videotape playing in the background: "This is making
me hot." Automatically, his hand reaches into his shorts. Ever the loyal
friend, Carpenter follows suit. For the remainder of the scene, the two
men combine their self-gratification with wisecracks and semi-serious
pronouncements about the difficulties of maintaining a relationship.
"What is it about women, Carpy?" Crane muses. "I mean, they tell you
one thing, and then they get you, and then they change their minds."
The scene ends with a medium-long shot of Carpenter and Crane sitting

on the sofa, intently watching their homemade porn. As we watch Crane watching himself while masturbating, we are reminded of Mishima's dream of being both seer and seen. In *Auto Focus,* the accomplishment of this desire leads not to an increase in reflexive self-awareness but a closed loop of exhibitionism and self-absorption.

Linda Ruth Williams describes the end of *Auto Focus,* when Crane is found alone in a hotel room bludgeoned to death with his own tripod, as a "morbid reworking of *Peeping Tom* [1960]" (Williams 33). The tools of the voyeur have been turned against him. While apt, this comparison overlooks one important difference. *Auto Focus* hinges on the pleasures and capacities of home video rather than film. The home video camera's proclivity to record anything and everything—from the once-in-a-lifetime event to the most banal family gathering—and its lack of separation between shooting and viewing make it the perfect accompaniment for Crane's narcissism. The grainy video images that replay Crane's sexual exploits record a performance that exists alongside rather than underneath the everyday "friendly guy" role. This coexistence of what remains irreconcilable links *Auto Focus* to the irreconcilable struggle between words and deeds in *Mishima,* the conflict between unbearable loneliness and violent rage in *Taxi Driver,* and, further back, to VanDorn's struggle to come to terms with his own actions and experiences in *Hardcore.* In each of these films, irreconcilability forms the core of the drama. The telling difference is the way it has gone from being a source of torment for the characters to being something barely registered, like a TV show left on while everyday life goes on all around it.

A Director for Hire

The ten years following the release of *Patty Hearst* are framed by Schrader's collaboration with Harold Pinter on the adaptation of Ian McEwan's novel *The Comfort of Strangers* (1990) and the critical success of Schrader's own adaptation of Russell Banks's novel *Affliction.* These years brought a number of changes in Schrader's career and in independent cinema more generally. In an interview coinciding with the release of *The Comfort of Strangers,* Schrader admitted: "I come from that film-school generation who probably put a little too much store by the idea of the writer-director. . . . But now I'm older, I feel like I'm probably a better director of other writers' material, and probably a better writer for other directors than I am for myself. With *Light of Day*, for instance, I was disappointed with my own script; I think I underestimated the value of that creative friction that can exist between a writer and a director" (qtd. in Banner 20).

By the time *The Comfort of Strangers* was released, Schrader had gone beyond the status of auteur-screenwriter achieved during the 1970s and had established himself as a leading writer-director. But as his comments indicate, this method of working was not without its own problems. Schrader's collaborations with Pinter and Banks provided a way out of the constrictions associated with his new role. These collaborations would be as important to Schrader's career in the 1990s as the collaborations with Scorsese and Scarfiotti were during the 1970s and early 1980s.

The other way the production circumstances of Schrader's films changed during this period relates to broader industry changes. Commencing with *Light of Day*, finance for Schrader's films was drawn from independent production companies based in either the United States or Europe, for example, Taft Entertainment Pictures (*Light of Day*), Atlantic Entertainment Group and Zenith Productions (*Patty Hearst*), and Erre Produzioni, Sovereign Pictures Productions, and Reteitalia (*The Comfort of Strangers*). During the 1980s, the rise in the number of independent production companies was a direct result of the demand for product generated by ancillary markets like home video and cable. The most successful of these companies—Carolco, Canon, DeLaurentis Entertainment Group, and Vestron—took on the status of mini-majors, putting together packages involving big-name stars, writers, and directors in much the same way as the larger studios. This approach meant there was often little difference between the types of films produced by the studios and those produced by independents. Those independent production companies that did try to provide an alternative came up against the perennial problem of distribution. Lacking name stars or large-budget effects on which to build their marketing campaigns, independent distributors faced immense difficulties in getting products recognized in a marketplace dominated by the distribution resources of the major studios. These difficulties often meant that, rather than gaining a theatrical release, a large number of independently produced films went straight to video.[9]

During the 1980s, Schrader's reputation as a writer-director and his willingness to work with small budgets meant that he was able to defy these industry pressures. In a survey of American filmmaking during the 1980s, Stephen Prince describes Schrader as "one of the decade's most interesting and intelligent filmmakers." He goes on to add: "The industry's ability to accommodate his unusual films says much about the institutional flexibility of the eighties and about the space open for unconventional filmmakers, partly as a result of the general need for product in the ancillary markets" (Prince 286). During the 1990s, the situation for independent cinema grew progressively worse. This decade saw a number of independent distribution companies taken over by large media conglomerates, for example, the purchase of Miramax by Disney/Capital Cities/ABC and Time Warner's acquisition of New Line. It was during this decade that the difficulty of securing distribution had its greatest impact on Schrader's films.

In a lead article in *Variety* in 1998, Andrew Hindes and Benedict Carver identify an oversupply of independently produced films unable to attract a distribution deal. At the top of a list of independently financed films that cost more than $5 million but were yet to acquire a distributor is *Affliction*. The authors quote Robert Corzo, the finance executive of Largo Entertainment, the production company responsible for *Affliction,* as bemoaning the lack of interest shown by the major studios: "The studios are concentrating on their tentpole movies. . . . No studio wants its staff to focus on an acquired movie instead of one that cost it $80 million to produce" (Hindes and Carver 87). Hindes and Carver note that the other reason why the major production companies are not interested in acquiring product from independent producers is their ability to source lower-budget "prestige product" directly from affiliate companies such as Miramax and New Line.

Commenting on this disappearing marketplace, Schrader observes: "With a few exceptions, there's no place for a $20 to $30 million movie anymore. . . . The movies that studios traditionally made for their prestige value have fallen to the independents, which of course are not so independent" (qtd. in Levy 505). Shut out from distribution, a number of small-to-medium-budget independent films ended up sold to cable, where they received their premiere before being released on video. Such was the fate of *Forever Mine*:

We showed the film around, and we got two distribution offers which were very low. The company that financed it was fighting to survive, and they thought that if they accepted one of those low offers it would expose their situation to the bankers, so they refused. They preferred to keep it on the shelf, let it die, than have to make that sale. It was a situation very similar to the one I had with *Affliction*. Eventually the company couldn't maintain the deception any longer, the banks and insurers were on to the fact that something was wrong and so they moved in to protect their interests, and the movie was sold to a cable channel. (*SOS* 261)

Schrader's frustration with the difficulties of raising financing and securing distribution resulted in his decision to direct *Witch Hunt* (1994) for HBO: "[E]ssentially, both *Witch Hunt* and *Touch* [1997] were reactions to my inability to get *Affliction* financed. With *Witch Hunt,* I was offered a job, and the notion of just making a film—of not having to talk actors into being in it and working for nothing and letting me use their name, and then going on for years trying to raise finance, and then finally making a film where you don't know whether or not it's going to get distribution . . ." (*SOS* 242).

Given these difficulties, Schrader's tenacity in dealing with the vagaries of film financing requires an equal degree of tenacity from the critic in responding not only to factors outside the director's control but also underlying themes, issues, and figures that recur across the films. While the 1990s brought enormous frustrations, the decade also resulted in three of Schrader's most important films: *The Comfort of Strangers, Light Sleeper,* and *Affliction.* These three films highlight Schrader's ability to interpret material drawn from elsewhere while also pursuing a distinct set of themes and characters from one film to the next—for example, *Light Sleeper*'s recasting of the central character in *Taxi Driver* and *American Gigolo.* And by the decade's end, this interplay between old and new, personal narratives and external influences, set a pattern that has carried through to the present.

Stories That Tell Us: *The Comfort of Strangers*

Looking back on this period in Schrader's career, a new tone or sensibility—described by one critic as an "almost introspective calm and an aching, melancholy impressionism" (Smith 50)—is evident. The first signs of this change appear in *The Comfort of Strangers*. The film begins with a series of extended tracking shots through the interior of a luxurious *palazzo*. The camera surveys the elaborate art works covering the walls and objects lying on desks and tables. The suggestion that the *palazzo* is some sort of museum is dispelled when one of the painted wall panels opens and a woman enters the room. Her entry coincides with the commencement of an unidentified male voice telling a story about a tyrannical father:

> My father was a very big man. All his life he wore a black moustache. When it turned grey he used a little brush to keep it black, such as ladies use for their eyes. Mascara.
>
> Everyone was afraid of him. My mother, my four sisters. At the dining table you could not speak unless spoken to first by my father.
>
> But he loved me. I was his favorite.

The care spent establishing this opulent world suggests that it will be central to the drama about to unfold. The initial purpose of the film's opening, however, is to act as the prologue to another story, about a young British couple on holiday in Venice. Mary (Natasha Richardson) and Colin (Rupert Everett) are trying to decide what to do about their relationship. An element of estrangement has crept into their interactions that takes the form of minor insults and irritations, for example, Mary's annoyance at Colin's patronizing response to her comments on visiting a church: "What's the point of saying that?" she asks him. "Why did you say that?" The young couple's holiday routine is interrupted when they wake from an afternoon nap to find that the nearby restaurants have closed. Without a map, they set off in search of a restaurant recommended by the concierge, and it is at this point that the two stories present in the film's opening—a story about the cruelty of the past and a story about a sense of estrangement in the present—commence their fatal intersection.

The disconcerting experience of trying to navigate the narrow alleyways of Venice has been explored by a number of filmmakers, for example, Luchino Visconti in *Senso* (1954) and Nicolas Roeg in *Don't Look Now* (1973). Schrader's version of Venice takes advantage of the city's postcard beauty and its capacity to appear prisonlike. Lost within its

The Comfort of Strangers: Colin (Rupert Everett)
and Mary (Natasha Richardson): careless
sightseers whose uncertain story becomes
caught up and consumed by a much darker story.

narrow alleys and streets, Mary and Colin are rescued by Robert (Christopher Walken), a Venetian gentleman who offers to take them to a bar that also serves excellent food. When they arrive at the bar, they discover the kitchen has closed. Robert asks them various questions about their relationship: Are they married? Do they have children? In turn, Colin and Mary ask Robert about his personal history: Where did he learn his excellent English? How did he meet his Canadian wife? He tells them that the only way to explain this is by first describing his mother and sisters: "And that would only make sense if I first described my father."

The story Robert tells is an extension of the story we heard at the start of the film. In this version, Robert describes how his relationship to his elder sisters, Maria and Eva, was forever changed by the consequences of an afternoon spent playing dress-up in their parents' bedroom. When Robert is unable to keep this activity a secret from his father, Eva and Maria are severely punished. A month later, the two girls exact their revenge. Pretending they want to make things right with their brother,

Maria and Eva present Robert with a feast of cooking chocolate, cream cake, marshmallows, and lemonade. Before gorging himself on these treats, Robert is told that he must fortify his stomach by drinking a foul-tasting medicine. When he finishes consuming all the sweets, Robert starts to feel nauseous and dizzy. Seizing their opportunity, Eva and Maria bind his hands with rope and lock him in their father's study where he vomits and defecates all over the carpets. On his return, Robert's father beats him and refuses to speak to his former favorite for six months. Robert's only solace is his mother: "I grew so thirsty at night. She brought me a glass of water every night and laid her hand upon my brow. . . . When my father was away I slept in her bed."

Robert's story jumps forward to the occasion of an afternoon tea with the wife and daughter of the Canadian ambassador. Left alone by the adults, Eva attempts to humiliate her brother by disclosing his habit of sleeping with his mother. Rather than joining in the sisters' ridicule, the ambassador's daughter smiles at Robert and states: "I think that's really awfully sweet." This act of kindness marks the first meeting of Robert and the person who would later become his wife.

On the trip back to their hotel, Mary and Colin once again lose their way. Nauseous from the combination of lack of food, strong wine, and the cruelty of Robert's story, Mary is sick in the canal. Unable to retrace their steps, the young couple spend the night sleeping against a wall waiting for daybreak. Despite their apparent dislike of Robert, this encounter is the first of a series of meetings. The next morning, Robert spots Colin and Mary at a café, and he convinces them that the best place to recover from their ordeal is not in the noisy hotel but in the peace and quiet of his luxurious *palazzo*. After catching up on lost sleep, Colin and Mary wake to find their clothes have been taken. When Mary goes in search of their clothes, she meets Caroline (Helen Mirren), Robert's wife. Caroline compliments Mary on Colin's beauty and confesses that while they were sleeping she crept into their room and watched them sleep. She jokes that their missing clothes will only be returned if they agree to stay for dinner.

While the dinner proceeds without incident, the antipathy that marks Colin's responses to Robert's conversation has its origins in a strange incident just prior to dinner. Robert is showing Colin the *palazzo*, inherited from his grandfather. He shows him various objects passed down from one generation of men to the next: books, old photos, a pair of opera glasses. "My father and his father understood themselves, clearly," he tells Colin. "They were men, and they were proud of their sex. Women understood them too. Now women treat men like children because they can't take them seriously. But men, like my father and grandfather, women took very seriously." Colin's response to Robert's reflections carries only a hint of derision: "So . . . this is a museum dedicated to the good old days?" It is Robert's reaction that catches us by surprise. Recalling a similar moment in Pinter's *The Birthday Party*, Robert punches Colin in the stomach. As Colin doubles over, Robert coolly lights a cigarette and winks at his stunned houseguest. The scene then cuts and we see the two couples seated at the dining table—almost as if nothing has happened. If not for Colin's hostile response to Robert's comments at dinner, we could be forgiven for thinking we had imagined the whole incident or that the film had imagined it for us out of the hints and subtext at work in the narrative.

Given what has already been revealed in the film, the question raised in the second half of *The Comfort of Strangers* is: Why do Colin and Mary return to Robert's *palazzo?* This is another way of asking: What is their complicity in the events that follow? "What did you want from these people?" the police detective asks Mary near the film's end. "So, why did you go to dinner? And why did you go back?" The detective's grilling of Mary echoes the courtroom interrogation in *Patty Hearst*. In both films, motivations are deliberately obscured. This refusal to spell out motivation initially attracted Schrader to Pinter's script:

> Pinter's characters are always saying one thing and meaning something slightly different. There are layers of nuance and innuendo and seemingly inexplicable actions and events which are in fact very explicable in a non-prosaic fashion. I'm very attracted to the idea of a psychological life running just under the surface of normal life and motivating the normal life in subtle ways: it goes back to why does Travis take the girl to the porno movie? It seemingly doesn't make sense, but of course it does make sense. (*SOS* 198)

In *The Comfort of Strangers*, the ambiguous relationship between the two couples creates a sense of strangeness as not only an external threat but as something closer to home. Robert and Caroline are not simply antagonists for the young couple. They are more like doppel-gängers or doubles. In his study of the double in nineteenth-century fiction, John Herdman argues that the double occupies an ambiguous position as "a second self, or *alter ego,* which appears as a distinct and separate being apprehensible by the physical senses (or at least, by *some* of them), but exists in a dependent relation to the original" (Herdman 14). Herdman emphasizes that this dependency does not mean that the double is subordinate, "for often the double comes to dominate, control, and usurp the functions of the subject." The sensation of being taken over or acceding to the view of another lies at the heart of Colin's odd question to Mary during dinner: "When people look at you and, well, you know, talk about your thighs and your bottom or both, etcetera—what sense of *your* thighs and *your* bottom do you, at such a time, have?"

The experience of subjective takeover implied in Colin's question is given a more sadistic rendering in the two fantasies that Mary and Colin tell each other during a pause in the lovemaking that follows their dinner with Robert and Caroline:

> MARY: I'm going to hire a surgeon—a very handsome surgeon—to cut off your arms and your legs. . . . And I'll keep you in a room in my house . . . and use you just for sex, whenever I feel like it. . . . And sometimes I'll lend you to my girlfriends, and they can do what they like with you. . . .
>
> COLIN: I'm going to invent a machine . . . made of steel, powered by electricity. It has controls, pistons, and there's straps, dials. It makes a low hum . . . like this. . . . And the machine will fuck you—not just for hours and days but for years and years and years and years. . . . Forever.

Where do these fantasies come from? It seems the story about a crisis within the relationship between Colin and Mary has been taken over and transformed through its encounter with another story. Just as Mary seems to replay the story told by Robert when she vomits in the canal, the sadomasochistic fantasies Mary and Colin tell each other are picked up and replayed in Caroline's tale of the violence that has come to dominate her sexual relations with Robert. She describes the changes in her responses to this violence. It was not the pain itself that Caroline found enjoyable, "But . . . somehow the fact of being helpless before it . . . being reduced to nothing by it." The sense of stories echoing across different contexts culminates when Mary's fantasy concerning the amputation of Colin's arms and legs receives grim realization in the couple's final encounter with Robert and Caroline. As Mary sits in a drugged stupor watching Robert cut Colin's throat, it is as if her fantasy has escaped the enclosure of the relationship and come to life in the form of a sadistic tableau staged especially for her. But now she is no longer a teller of the story but a passive witness to the telling.

Stories, impulses, and feelings that pass from one context to the next, from one couple to the next, are part of the logic of interpersonal engagement played out in *The Comfort of Strangers*. Drifting through the city, uncertain of what they are doing or why they have come in the first place, Colin and Mary become defined as a couple through their interpolation in the story that overarches and, for Robert at least, explains all the other stories in the film: the story of Robert's relationship to his father. We first hear this story near the start of the film as a disembodied voiceover. This is the same story Robert retells and carries forward at the bar after he rescues Colin and Mary. It is also the story Robert begins to tell the bewildered detectives at the very end of the film. We might see certain details in the story as evidence of a flaw in the father's masculine demeanor, for example, the distinctly feminine habit of using a little brush to paint mascara on his greying moustache.[10] And there is no doubt that Colin stirs in Robert deep feelings of attraction and repulsion that have their origins in the exaggerated masculinity of his father.

But in understanding the significance of Robert's story, it is crucial to heed not only the story's details but also the compulsive manner of its retelling. In its pattern of repetition and retelling, *The Comfort of Strangers* recalls the process of repetition that bedevils Michael in *Obsession*. In both films, characters are taken over by stories that they are helpless to control. This is why, when Robert retells the story in the bar, the camera does something that at first appears strange: it drifts away from the person telling the story to scrutinize other inhabitants of the bar. Why not? Unlike the young couple, the camera has heard this story before. The story Robert tells has been told already and will be told again—not only by him but also by all those with whom he comes in contact. In this sense, the story exists independently of the characters who are part of its telling—just as the space created by the camera insists on its independence. This is why the final word in the film does not belong to Robert but to the story he is compelled to tell over and over again. The story *tells* him. "Listen," he says to the detectives. "Let me tell you something. . . . My father was a very big man. All his life he wore a black moustache. When it turned grey, he used a little brush to keep it black, such as ladies use. Mascara."

The Comfort of Strangers thus marks an important stylistic advance and the consolidation of a particular type of story working its way through Schrader's films: a story about the self's capacity to be taken over and made not its own. This capacity serves as the dramatic tipping point in so many of Schrader's films. That the consolidation of this story comes about through the words of others—Pinter and McEwan—affirms the logic of interpersonal engagement explored in *The Comfort of Strangers*. The other figure central to the consolidation

The Comfort of Strangers: For Robert (Christopher Walken), Colin is both an object of desire and threat to the monolithic masculinity that he associates with his father.

of Schrader's story in *The Comfort of Strangers* is Bertolucci. In various interviews, Schrader acknowledges his borrowings of scenes and stylistic devices from *The Conformist*. In *The Comfort of Strangers*, Bertolucci's use of an unmotivated camera provides Schrader with a model for a different style of storytelling, in which the primacy of the central character is under question:

> By and large, in the first half of the history of movies the camera moved as action or character dictated; it moved to follow a character, it moved to lead with an action, and so on. But starting with Bertolucci we see a really strong case of the unmotivated camera, the camera moved on its own. If [Jean-Louis] Trintignant was walking away from you in the hallway, the camera might be pulling back rather than following him, and if he was in one room the camera might move over to the next room and wait for him to come rather than move when he did. (*SOS* 211)

In *The Conformist*, the disconcerting jumps between past and present, the monumental style of the Fascist-period architecture, and the detachment of the camera from the central character evoke the alienated nature of Marcello's (Jean-Louis Trintignant) desire to build a normal life. Compromised by his guilt concerning a boyhood homosexual encounter, Marcello is incapable of responding to the events that determine his fate. In the film's famous climax, he sits huddled in a car while the woman he loves is being murdered by Fascist thugs—a murder that he has helped to orchestrate. "[T]he character has become a kind of viewer," writes Gilles Deleuze. "He shifts, runs and becomes animated in vain, the situation he is in outstrips his motor capacities on all sides, and makes him see and hear what is no longer subject to the rules of a response or an action" (Deleuze, *Cinema 2* 3). Deleuze's description of changes in postwar European cinema provides a useful point of connection between films like *The Conformist* and Schrader's own desire to represent character differently—not simply as a determining narrative agent but as acted on by forces he or she is unable to comprehend. The form of Schrader's films—their emphasis on high-design settings, the independence of the camera, and the prominent role of music—needs to be read as a consequence of this fundamental recasting.

Lost Souls: *Light Sleeper*

As they are leaving the *palazzo* after having dinner, Mary stops to look at a pile of photographs lying on Robert's desk. In the last photograph, we catch a glimpse of Colin's image. Mary's expression registers that she also recognizes Colin in the photograph. Nothing is said of this incident until some time later when, after waking from a nightmare, Mary tells Colin that one of the photographs in Robert's apartment was of him. Mary's panicked response seems to intuit the danger represented in the photograph. She touches Colin's neck—as if checking for signs of the wound that we later see on his lifeless body in the morgue. Despite Mary's urgings, Colin drifts back to sleep. It is only the following day that Mary's story registers with Colin. As they are lying on the beach, he tells Mary about Robert's physical attack. That Mary and Colin keep their strange experiences a secret until some time after the event suggests that neither knows exactly what to make of them. Something important has happened; as yet, however, neither character knows what it might mean. The meaning of these strange events only occurs after the fact.

Meanings and insights arriving late also underpin the tone of introspection running through *Light Sleeper*. As he enters the fourth decade of his life, John LeTour (Willem Dafoe) faces some important decisions. Until now he has been happy to work as a delivery boy for Ann (Susan Sarandon), a mid-level Manhattan drug dealer specializing in "white drugs for white people." But with Ann preparing to move out of drug dealing and into the cosmetics business, LeTour has to think about other ways to make a living. His vague plan—"I'm gonna get into recording"—barely masks his anxiety about the future. When change comes for LeTour, it is the culmination of a number of different events, coincidences, and suspicions: a police investigation into the overdose of a wealthy college girl in a park; a chance encounter between LeTour and his former lover, Marianne (Dana Delany); a psychic's warning of betrayal; and a terrible collision between past and present lives during the course of one of LeTour's drug deliveries. LeTour's desperate attempt to make sense of all these things draws a line under his life in the drug trade. His consolation is to be able to take Ann's hand in the visitors' room of the prison and tentatively look forward to the future. At the end of *Light Sleeper,* change comes for all the characters—whether they like it or not, whether they are ready for it or not.

The final close-up of LeTour's face resting against Ann's hand replays the final shot of *American Gigolo,* when Julian leans his head against the glass separating him from Michelle. In *Light Sleeper,* this is one of a number of allusions linking the central character not only to the protagonist in *American Gigolo* but also to Travis Bickle in *Taxi Driver.* The opening low-angle shot of a city street illuminated by the headlights of a car and the clouds of steam rising from the road suggest that these

Light Sleeper: John LeTour (Willem Dafoe) enacts one of the key archetypes in Schrader's films from the 1990s: the light sleeper.

are the same streets traveled by Travis. While the anger and rage associated with the earlier film may no longer be present, what remains is the character's introspection.

Schrader wrote *Light Sleeper* as the third stage of the life journey that began with Travis in *Taxi Driver:* "When he was in his twenties he was very hostile and paranoid and was a cab driver. Then in his thirties he was very narcissistic and self-involved and he was a gigolo. And now he's forty, he's . . . anxious. He hasn't made anything of his life, . . . and he's a drug delivery boy" (qtd. in Jackson, "Blood" 24). These associations and connections draw us in by suggesting a past not literally that of the character or the film but one that works according to a logic of resemblance and similarity. And just as the films taken together weave a fabric of common obsessions, similarities, and echoes, within *Light Sleeper* we find a drama less about a clearly defined event than something harder to define: reflection, memory, yearning, an inability to look forward—in short, a stubborn, obsessive melancholy.

In his essay on film noir, Schrader describes how this inability to look forward gives rise to a particular type of cinematic mannerism: "[T]here is a passion for the past and present, but a fear of the future. The *noir* hero dreads to look ahead, but instead tries to survive by the day, and if unsuccessful at that, he retreats to the past. Thus *film noir's* techniques emphasize loss, nostalgia, lack of clear priorities, insecurity; then submerge these self-doubts in mannerism and style" (*SOS* 86). In *Light Sleeper,* Schrader models the form of the film around these same sentiments. LeTour's anxiety about the future finds expression in the ramblings that he jots down in his diary:

> Labor Day weekend. Some time for a garbage strike. Everybody crazy to stock up. They decide to score at the last minute and they want it now. Never fails. The faces look alike. You gotta use memory tricks: each one has some peculiarity—it keeps you sharp. A D.D. told me when a drug dealer starts writing a diary it's time to quit. I started writing after that. Not every night. Now and then. Fill up one book, throw it out, start another.

As LeTour travels through the city, the lights of passing vehicles play across his face in a way that destabilizes its contours and presence. His view on the world is detached yet laden with nostalgia. Like Julian's hustle in *American Gigolo,* LeTour's actions simulate a form of social contact that allows him to get the job done and move away untouched. To find a reason for his survival in the drug business, LeTour places great store in the notion of luck: "You're walking down the street, some guy that looks maybe a little like you does a stick-up four hours ago, and a cop pulls you in 'cause he's cold and wants to go inside—they grab your stash. Your number's up. You're busted for nothing. For bad luck."

The first indication that LeTour's luck is changing—for good or ill— occurs when he catches sight of his former lover, Marianne, during a rainy evening. She accepts his offer of a lift but remains wary. Four years of sobriety and a determination to avoid the company of former drug associates ensure that the encounter is brief. For LeTour, the encounter means something. Back in his apartment, he pours over snapshots of his former life with Marianne, running his finger along the contours of her face. The next day he visits a psychic. Astrological charts, psychic readings, and New Age spirituality are a key part of the milieu in which LeTour circulates. This is a world held together by a mix of hard-edged commercial imperatives and the last vestiges of belief in alternative spirituality. While this world is cluttered with potential meanings, the central character finds that he is drifting further and further away from the possibility of insight. "I'm thirty-eight years old," LeTour tells the psychic. "Forty. . . . I have trouble sleeping. . . . What is around me? Is it dark? Have I run out of luck? Is there luck for me?" The psychic warns LeTour that a woman close to him will betray him. Although this never eventuates, it is one more undercurrent in the confluence of events that fuel LeTour's anxiety.

Signs of luck, coincidences, unexplained meetings: LeTour's sense of things changing is reinforced shortly after his meeting with the psychic. One of Ann's valued clients, Tis (Victor Garber), has called from the hospital desperately in need of sedatives to calm his nerves prior to being interviewed by the police about an overdose victim. As LeTour is walking through the hospital corridors, he bumps into Marianne's sister, who is caring for her dying mother. When Marianne steps into the corridor, she just manages to contain her unease at the sight of LeTour. After some coaxing, Marianne agrees to LeTour's offer to buy her a coffee from the cafeteria. When they sit down, Marianne again refuses to tell LeTour anything about her current life: "Details just open the door." With no place to go, the conversation inevitably turns to the past. LeTour sees the past as a "magical" time marked by passion and romance. Marianne remembers it differently: "You took off for three months without telling me and called once. That's how magical we were. You were an encyclopedia of suicidal fantasies—I heard every one. I mean, nobody could clear a room like you, John. And the friends, you may have noticed, turned out to be mine, not yours. I envy you. A convenient memory is a gift from God."

Schrader films the conversation between the former lovers by alternating over-the-shoulder shots of each speaker with two-shots of the couple positioned at either end of the frame. Toward the end of the conversation, this setup is disrupted by a cut to a shot on the other side of a large rectangular pylon, thus reversing the position of the characters and bringing the pylon into the foreground. During the shooting, the trigger for this formal rearrangement was Schrader's recollection of a Merle Haggard song: "Between Your Life and Mine There's a Wall I Can't See Through." The cut to the other side of the pylon allows Schrader to literalize the metaphor. Viewed in terms of the film's broader implications, the camera's abrupt relocation has other meanings. Just as the significance of the past cannot be made to conform to a single point of view, the staging of the central relationship is also open to a sudden change of perspective. The intrusion of the pylon is a blunt reminder of the scene's contingency and a way of telling the story through the spaces and settings surrounding the characters.

The interplay between camera and setting is even more pronounced in the next scene, when the camera follows LeTour to a nightclub. The scene begins with a long shot of LeTour arriving at the club. The camera tracks behind him as he enters the club and pauses while he takes his bearings. When LeTour spots his clients and moves toward their table, the camera cranes toward the ceiling, where its attention falls on an elaborate mural. Maybe the answer to Marianne's reappearance can be found in the mural, or maybe in the words of Michael Been's song that Schrader foregrounds at this point. Ranging from a series of breathy sighs and moans to more conventionally sung lyrics, the soundtrack provides "another voice" on the action: "I'd toyed around in the past . . . with having a kind of ballad structure, where you have a singer who is sort of telling a tale behind your back, which is like the tale you're seeing"

Light Sleeper: Marianne (Dana Delany) and LeTour
wrestle with the meaning of the past.

(Schrader qtd. in Smith 51). Although we may not always understand what Been is singing, the fragments of lyrics we do catch—"Maybe I'll see better when the storm has passed"—contribute to this sense of a narrative forming just behind our back.

After a few seconds, the camera descends and reconnects with Le-Tour chatting with his clients and transacting business. "The camera isn't necessarily motivated by the action," Schrader's cameraman Ed Lachman tells us, "it's used in a more psychological way. Let's say that sometimes we use the camera at a higher angle to LeTour, so you feel a sense of oppression because the camera's above the eye line. And sometimes the camera will draw away from the character, to situate him in his environment or comment on his relationship with it" (qtd. in Jackson, "Blood" 26). Interestingly, Lachman states that the inspiration for this approach was drawn from watching Antonioni's films from the 1960s, such as *La Notte* (1961), *L'Eclisse* (1962), and *Red Desert* (1964). In these films, the camera's attention constantly shifts between the characters and the physical world in which they are immersed. In *L'Eclisse*, for example, the camera's framing of the central character, Vittoria (Monica Vitti), allows us to consider the alterations of her emotional state and the material reality that surrounds her and exists independent of her presence. Gilberto Perez describes this as a particular form of distracted attention: "Nothing happens in such scenes except an experience of awareness, awareness of the world and of the self in transaction with the world" (Perez 19).

In *Light Sleeper*, also, we can find this sense of a productive distraction. On a number of occasions, Schrader either ends or begins a scene by holding on the shot of an object, for example, the statue of Beatrice as LeTour is leaving Ann's apartment; or the carefully composed arrangement of cutlery and dessert bowls at the start of the scene between Ann and LeTour at the fancy restaurant. A more overt registering of an object world surrounding the central character occurs when Marianne and LeTour make love in her hotel room. The camera cranes down from the ceiling to frame the couple as they kneel on the bed facing each other. Directly behind Marianne's shoulder, a large mural of Jan Vermeer's *The Lacemaker* seems to keep watch over the scene.

In *Light Sleeper*, it is not that milieu and character have become independent of each other; it is more that the character has a tendency to become secondary to other activities and points of interest that grab the camera's attention. The camera seems to know something that LeTour has also come to divine: it will have to make its own way through a world that, little by little, is pulling away and leaving us behind. The notebooks that LeTour fills up and then discards testify to an accumulation of events and experiences lacking a connecting thread. Piles of garbage gathering on the streets, empty wine bottles, experiences, memories, and moods—one on top of the other, marking an unknown contiguity and a kind of psychic paralysis.

False Events: *Affliction*

LeTour's desperation for answers comes to a head when he again bumps into Marianne, this time at Tis's apartment. Marianne's strung-out appearance indicates the toll taken by her mother's death. Earlier, Marianne had turned on LeTour: "Every time you come into my life something terrible happens. I thought I was rid of you." As he is about to get into the car, LeTour hears a terrible scream. When he walks

Light Sleeper: LeTour and Marianne: figures in a
world of competing points of attention.

back to the front of the building, he sees Marianne's body face-down
on the footpath. Did she jump? Was she pushed? Is Marianne's death
related to the death of the college girl in the park? Is Tis the common
factor that brings these things together? Given that these questions are
beyond LeTour's capacity to provide answers, it is inevitable that when
he decides to act, the outcome is a strangely dissociated presentation
of violence reminiscent of the infamous bloodbath at the end of *Taxi
Driver*. At the end of the scene, LeTour eases himself onto the hotel
bed. In a frontal medium close-up, the camera frames his wounded body.
LeTour looks directly at the camera and slowly falls back on the bed.
As LeTour disappears from view, the camera holds for a brief moment
on the shot of a Chinese print above the bed—one more mystery in a
world already overcrowded with potential significance.

It is part of the nature of the story told in *Light Sleeper* that we
have been here before and most likely will be here again. This sense of
repetition is part of a pattern of storytelling based around acts of mis-
understanding and estrangement. *The Comfort of Strangers* initiated
new ways of telling this story. The freedom given to the camera and the

attention paid to setting in this film fed directly into the telling of the story in *Light Sleeper*. In turn, *Light Sleeper*'s mood of melancholy had a crucial influence on Schrader's adaptation of Joseph Connelly's novel *Bringing Out the Dead* for Scorsese. Here, too, we find a way of life carried on *post facto*. Like LeTour, Frank Pierce (Nicolas Cage), the central character in *Bringing Out the Dead*, is a type of zombie. Unable to get himself fired from his job as a paramedic, Frank hurtles from one disaster scene to the next, hoping to redeem his guilt and sense of failure by saving a life. Despite his hunger for redemption, Frank admits that he is simply a "grief mop": someone bearing witness to other people's tragedies. His feelings of guilt and failure coalesce in the face of a young girl whose life he should have saved but didn't. Wherever he goes, he sees the dead girl's face superimposed on the faces of the hooded street urchins that stare back at him in the ambulance.

Taken collectively, *The Comfort of Strangers*, *Light Sleeper*, and *Bringing Out the Dead* remind us how much Schrader's scripts and films revolve around questions of experience: the struggle to make sense of people and things, in the present and the past. As a notion, experience is about this capacity of past and present to coexist and how this coexistence has a bearing on each step we take and each relationship we seek to develop, maintain, or in some way understand. But there is something else running through Schrader's films: a sense that we can become subject to experiences that cannot be fully understood, experiences whose impact becomes noticeable in retrospect when it is too late to do anything about it. These experiences do not make us wiser or bring us closer together but highlight a sense of incommensurability. Such is the fate of many of Schrader's characters who find themselves claimed by experience. The issue for Schrader is how to convey this notion of subjective experience while also heeding other necessities such as genre, plot tension, and narrative resolution. Or, put another way, how to create characters that are central to the drama yet no longer at the center of the story. "Experience is neither true nor false," writes Michel Foucault, "it is always a fiction, something constructed, which exists only after it has been made, not before; it isn't something that is 'true,' but it has been a reality" (Foucault 36). As Foucault notes, the issue of experience is inseparable from issues of narration and storytelling. This is not to denounce experience as false; it is rather to consider the role of storytelling in its construction.

The struggle to narrate experience underpins the drama in *Affliction*. As in *Light Sleeper,* the central narrative event in this film is a false event: a series of connections between people and events that exist only in the imagination of the central character. "[T]he thing I loved, was that it was a story pretending to be something else: sort of meandering around, leading you to believe that a murder mystery was afoot. And then, in the book and in the film, about two-thirds of the way through, you realize that there was no murder, and that this is a character study, and this man has gone crazy" (*SOS* 254). In place of a murder mystery, *Affliction* offers a drama of fathers and sons, brothers and best friends, the places they occupy, and the stories they tell or are unable to tell about each other.

It begins quietly enough. The opening credits are accompanied by a series of images set against a black background—a wire fence line leading to houses in the distance, a mobile home with a police car parked out front, a street scene, a garage—all of which are blanketed by snow with only the slightest indication of movement to indicate that these images are not indeed photographs. Each image remains on screen just long enough for us to register its content and some of the smaller details before fading out to be replaced by another image. While they mean little to us as yet, the careful way these images are framed and presented demands that we pay close attention. "Look and see," the film seems to say, "it was right here in this place, in this house and on these streets that the events we are about to watch happened. They could not have happened anywhere else." Although there are no people inhabiting these images, their rhetoric is unmistakably that of a family album: a memorial record, as André Bazin once wrote, "of lives halted at a set moment in their duration" (Bazin 14).

The final image in this series is of a country road at night, an image that gradually enlarges to fill the screen. As we watch this image enlarge, an offscreen voice—resonant and familiar—starts to speak at almost the same time that a set of headlights appear. Guiding these headlights is the afflicted figure of Wade, the subject of the tale. "This is the story of my older brother's strange criminal behavior and disappearance. We who loved him no longer speak of Wade. It's as if he never existed. . . . By telling his story like this, by breaking the silence about him, I tell my own story as well. Everything of importance, that is, everything that gives rise to the telling of this story, occurred during a single deer-hunting season in a small town in upstate New Hampshire where Wade was raised and so was I."

In "The Storyteller," Walter Benjamin offers a beautiful description of how traditional storytelling, unlike information or a report, "does not aim to convey the pure essence of the thing" it describes: "It sinks the thing into the life of the storyteller, in order to bring it out of him again. Thus traces of the storyteller cling to the story the way the handprints of the potter cling to the clay vessel" (Benjamin 91–92). In *Affliction*, the opening words establish not only the particular tense of the tale and the filial relationship between the narrator, Rolfe (Willem Dafoe), and the protagonist, Wade, but also the outline of a deep complicity between storyteller and the thing he describes. "The story is really about him telling the story," Schrader proposes. "In the book this aspect is much clearer because everything is seen through the narrator's eyes. He's telling you about events that he's only surmising, because he's talked to people in the town" (Bliss 8). How do we understand this complicity between Rolfe and the story he is telling? What is the nature of the relationship that binds the two brothers together in the tragic events that occurred in this small New Hampshire town?

It is Rolfe who puts together the scenario that transforms the hunting accident involving one of Wade's closest friends, Jack Hewitt (Jim True), and Evan Twombley (Sean McCann), the union official, into a murder conspiracy. It is also Rolfe who, after the funeral of their mother, rekindles Wade's flagging commitment to this version of events. And in the end, Rolfe is the one left behind, the one obligated to tell this story over and over again. But the complicity between Rolfe and Wade extends beyond these narrative details, back to their shared history of childhood and their traumatic relationship to their father (James Coburn). This is another way of saying that the story being told by Rolfe is not just any story, something that happens all of a sudden or out of the blue—in this instance, the story of an accident that comes to be seen as a conspiracy. It is also, and primarily, a story about the past and how it leaves its mark in the form of either physical or emotional bruises. "I was a careful child," Rolfe tells Wade during one of their conversations. "I became a careful adult." Almost as an afterthought, he adds: "At least I was never afflicted by that man's violence." These words hang in the air momentarily. Wade's response—when it comes—is couched in laughter yet no less devastating: "That's what *you* think."

Already we can say this much about the story being told in *Affliction:* more than a set of challenges or forces that act upon the characters and which they respond to in turn, the story is also constituted by an ever-present relationship to the past. In *Light Sleeper,* there is also a sense of an all-pervading past: LeTour's past relationship with Marianne, but also a past lifestyle that both characters are unable to escape. Asked about the particular need met by the making of the film, Schrader replies: "It's a coming to terms with one's own encroaching nostalgia as you get older, the temptation of thinking that it was better before. . . . And then that nostalgia starts to bleed into relationships and self-identity, and you become kind of a backward-thinking person" (qtd. in Smith 54). In the final scene of *Light Sleeper,* LeTour asks Ann: "Did we ever fuck?" Although it initially gives rise to another round of remembrance, LeTour's blunt question also serves to chart a way forward: "I was thinking about it, and I realized we never really did. It's one of the things I think about. One of the things I look forward to." Age is catching up with Schrader's characters, but it does not bring with it wisdom or clarity about the past. The best that *Light Sleeper* can offer these characters is a sense of resignation. This is captured in the film's final line, spoken by Ann: "Strange how things work."

In *Affliction,* the past functions more prosaically, so prosaically that it seems Wade is able to encounter his past—or a version of it, at least—floating just out of earshot as the central narrative of a barfly's conversation. Wade's relationship to his father has become part of the folklore of the community, part of the public process by which the community tells stories about itself and its inhabitants. Wade listens to the story coming from the other side of the bar as if it were the story of someone close, someone he knows and recognizes yet from whom he is fundamentally removed. In *Affliction,* recognition and estrangement work hand in hand. They are part of the same response to a past that one can neither simply embrace nor reject.

Affliction: Wade (Nick Nolte) listening to the story of his past being told in the bar.

In this film, the past is like a habit or way of responding that binds one to certain places, people, and forms of behavior: a type of social inheritance that *claims us.* "I didn't hit him," Wade assures Lillian (Mary Beth Hurt), his ex-wife, after losing his temper with her new husband. "I'm not going to hit anybody." The claims of the past are also present in the way Wade and his father—in spite of the antipathy and violence—are slowly yet inevitably drawn together in a strange kind of pact that leaves no room for other characters. After his mother's death, Wade moves into his father's house with his girlfriend, Margie Fogg (Sissy Spacek). He starts drinking from the various bottles hidden around the place. We see him lash out and explode in paroxysms of rage at his father, his sore tooth, and his poor treatment by Lillian. In between these outbursts, he experiences moments of painful self-awareness. Unable to sleep, he wanders over to the dressing table and catches his reflection in the mirror: "I glanced up, and there he was. Only it was me. But it was like I'd never seen myself before. It was a . . . stranger's face." This stranger's face is the clearest sign of the father's legacy and one more manifestation of the internal disquiet that pulls at Schrader's characters. As we watch

Wade sit at his father's table in the film's final moments, quietly sipping Brown's Canadian whisky, it is clear that the physical resemblance between the actors—Nick Nolte and James Coburn—stands in for a much deeper resemblance and complicity.

Logic of Betrayal

In *Light Sleeper*, LeTour is told to watch out for a betrayal that never eventuates. In *Affliction*, betrayal is central to the relationship between the two brothers. "You will say that I should have known terrible things were about to happen. You will say that I was responsible. But even so, what could I have done by then?" For Schrader, Rolfe's supplication—both acknowledging and deflecting responsibility—marks the dramatic heart of the film: "You have in this case two siblings of an abusive parent. One of those siblings will be selected out for the violence, in this case the older one. . . . [O]n one hand [Rolfe is] very grateful that his brother took the blows for him. On the other hand, he's jealous, because in that kind of family structure, violence equals attention equals love" (qtd. in Joyce). Is Wade another in the long line of male heroes identified by Adrian Martin who "find themselves duped by those closest to them—not merely those least suspected, but those most totally and blindly trusted"? Martin adds, "This is the larger, more brilliant, and certainly more evil form of betrayal—the betrayal that exploits love, the sweet cheat" (Martin, *Once* 41).

Rolfe's betrayal of Wade in *Affliction*—if one could even call it that—is certainly less overt than the scenarios Martin has in mind. It is hardly a betrayal at all; perhaps more a barely conscious act of exploitation and abuse that, like all the other acts of emotional and physical abuse in the film, contains its own momentum and afterlife. "Jesus, Rolfe! Don't you care about what's right?" Wade demands after Rolfe coolly lays out his theory of what really happened to Twombley during the hunting trip. "I care about what happened," Rolfe replies. "The truth. And remember, I'm a student of history." For someone who describes himself as being a careful adult, the apparent carelessness with which Rolfe feeds Wade's anger is utterly extraordinary. So extraordinary, in fact, that it is hard not to read into his actions the latent resentment and jealousy that Schrader describes so well.

Affliction: Wade with his father, Glen (James Coburn), and his brother, Rolfe (Willem Dafoe), at his mother's funeral. Standing behind the men are Wade's sister, Lena (Martha-Marie Kleinhans), and Wade's partner, Margie Fogg (Sissy Spacek).

And as we listen to Rolfe lay out his theory of what actually happened during the hunting trip, something else becomes apparent about the relationship of the two brothers and the type of story being told. Referring to the writings of Eric Rohmer and Claude Chabrol on Hitchcock, Deleuze proposes, "One does not commit a crime in Hitchcock, one delivers it up, one gives it or one exchanges it" (Deleuze, *Cinema 1* 201). In *I Confess* (1953), the murderer confesses to the crime and passes it on within the sanctified realm of the holy confessional. "[T]he criminal has always done his crime *for* another, . . . for the innocent man who, whether we like it or not, is innocent no longer" (201). Rather than any simple contrast between innocence and guilt, Hitchcock's concern is with the set of relations that surround the action. The exchange or offering up of the crime is the means by which these relations take on a dramatic momentum. In *Affliction,* we also have a crime that is delivered up, in this instance from brother to brother. Rolfe's careless speculations become a trigger for the actual crime, a crime surrounded and determined in advance of its occurrence by a series of relations spanning the present lives of the characters and their shared history.

An event happening in advance of itself and outside its proper time is the logic of action in Hitchcock's films. But it also resembles something central to the narrative in *Affliction:* the logic of trauma. In Sigmund Freud's writings it is not simply that the meaning of traumatic events are lost to time. Rather, they are bound to a temporal logic in which origins are displaced by a radiation of meaning and affect both forward and back across the history of the subject. The traumatized, Cathy Caruth goes as far as to argue, "become themselves the symptom of a history that they cannot entirely possess" (Caruth 5). These difficult histories generate a type of compulsive storytelling that Schrader also explored in *The Comfort of Strangers* and *Obsession.* In *Affliction,* the shooting of Jack by Wade, like the imaginary murder of Twombley that it follows and seeks to avenge, is itself one more instance in the retelling of a traumatic history circulating between the two brothers and their father. So too are Rolfe's desperate acts of denial about his place in this history: "It wasn't me," he tells Wade about a violent incident involving their father. "I wasn't there. I heard about it. When I heard about it, it was Elborn." These unstable relations between past and present, rather than any animosity between Wade and Jack, determine the meaning of the final killing.

There is something inexorable about this logic of repetition and replaying: kin follows kin, violence follows violence. "You Goddamn son of a bitch," Wade's father spits out as he stands over Wade. "I know you. You're my blood. You're a Goddamn fucking piece of my heart." At the end of the film, the fire that consumes the father's dead body seems a direct manifestation of the fire produced by the alcohol that has determined his relationship to his family. As Wade sits drinking at the table, watching the barn burn to the ground, it is unclear whether he has mastered his father's lesson in violence or found a way of escaping this affliction through an act at once brutal and self-immolating. What stands out as we watch this disaster unfold is the way that everything in this cinematic landscape carries with it the heaviness or weight of something that has been dispersed across a range of different transferences and relations—from the inside to the outside, from the past to the present, and from character to milieu.

Affliction: Glen Whitehouse acknowledges his son:
"You're a Goddamn fucking piece of my heart."

Nocturnal Wanderers

In *Affliction*, both brothers forsake the replenishment offered by sleep
for the sake of what Maurice Blanchot describes as "nocturnal wandering" (Blanchot 265). The nocturnal wanderer, or light sleeper, is a
recognizable figure across Schrader's films: from Travis in *Taxi Driver* to
LeTour in *Light Sleeper* and Frank in *Bringing Out the Dead*, we deal
with characters unable to rest, unable to renounce the day—characters
who, in Blanchot's words, "appear more or less guilty. What do they
do? They make night present" (265). Overburdened by memory, by the
past, and by a consciousness that refuses to shut down and "blot out
the night," these characters spend their time fabulating stories, making
connections, filling out diaries, and, in LeTour's case, scribbling odd
lists: people whose eyes don't match up, people who are left-handed.
In *Affliction*, Wade turns his inability to sleep into a series of late-night
phone calls to Rolfe in which he casts and recasts his resentment. For
Wade, as for the other characters, it is a question of how to make sense
of experience—how to contain it and put it to bed.

"Whoever does not sleep cannot stay awake," Blanchot helpfully reminds us (265). And it is true that in *Affliction,* an overwhelming sense of fatigue seems to hang over the characters. This fatigue needs to be understood in its everyday sense of all-pervading tiredness—for instance, the way Wade trudges slowly back up the steps of the town center after losing another fight with Lillian, or the way his body slumps forward in the snowplow as he clears the snowbound streets. But fatigue also needs to be understood as something more than a physical manifestation, something closer to the way it is used in Jean Epstein's early writings on cinema. As Stuart Liebman notes, fatigue signifies "a kind of physiological modification . . . in which active exploration of the external world by the intellect was supplanted by more introspective ruminations" (Liebman 190). For Epstein, fatigue is photogenic because it is a state of being marked by habit and routine. Moreover, it is universally experienced: "Everyone is a connoisseur, . . . there are no amateurs. We are all erudite and professional scholars of fatigue, neurasthenic esthetes" (Epstein 192). Fatigue marks a world in which time manifests itself through repetition: one day after another, one battle or personal slight after another. As Lillian puts it, with all her anger and disappointment at Wade, "You amaze me. Year after year in the same old ways." "Nolte's body," observes Charles Taylor in one of the best descriptions of the film, "seems to be a clock winding down before our eyes, a burden he's dragging around, a repository for each new resentment" (Taylor).

In a world burdened by repetition, routine, and destinies passed on from father to son, the only way to break out is through an action or act of violence that does not change the situation but rebounds on the one who commits it. At the end of the film, Wade isn't arrested. He isn't killed. He simply disappears. One moment, he is lighting a cigarette after shooting Jack. The next, he is gone—consigned to history. In Rolfe's final voiceover, he tries to account for the type of history that swallowed up his brother—a history based not on facts but on what Rolfe terms a "tradition of male violence" handed down from father to son:

> Wade killed Jack . . . just as surely as Jack did not kill Evan Twombley— even accidentally. The link between Jack and Twombley, LaRiviere, and Mel Gordon existed only in Wade's wild imaginings and briefly, I admit, in mine as well. . . . LaRiviere and Mel Gordon were indeed in business. The Parker Mountain ski resort is now advertised across the country.

The community of Lawford, as such, no longer exists. It is an economic zone between Littleton and Catamont. The house is still in Wade's name, and I keep paying taxes on it. It remains empty. Now and then I drive out there and sit in my car and wonder: "Why not let it go? Why not let LaRiviere buy it and build the condominiums he wants there?" We want to believe Wade died that same November, froze to death on a bench or a sidewalk. You cannot understand how a man, a normal man, a man like you and me can do such a terrible thing. Unless the police happen to arrest a vagrant who turns out to be Wade Whitehouse, there will be no more mention of him or his friend Jack Hewitt or our father. The story will be over . . . except . . . that I continue.

Rolfe's words continue the odd dance between complicity and denial, recognition and estrangement that marks his relation to the story he tells. The grainy low-resolution images taken from inside the house in the final scene were earlier used to represent Wade's memories of the past. Now we are in the present or, more precisely, in the aftermath of Wade's actions. Although the house is empty of human habitation, everything else is still in place: the beds have been made, the photographs are still on the wall, and all the furniture is in its proper place. Even the woollen cap lying next to the gloves and newspapers on the dining-room table could perhaps have been left there by Wade sometime before the terrible event. The camera moves over these objects, taking stock of what remains: the clues to a crime without mystery. After traveling down the stairs, it comes to rest near the table where Wade sat drinking his whisky and watching the barn burn. Outside the window we can see the charred remains of the barn and a group of small figures moving around the wreckage.

Everything about this final scene—its graininess, the movement of the camera, and its scrutiny of objects and surfaces—seems designed to reinforce a sense that, despite everything, despite all that we have seen and now know about the family that lived in this place, something still remains that refuses to give way to the inexorable logic of economic zones and property redevelopment. Rolfe's refusal to sell the family property to LaRiviere is not simply a resistance to the promise of a quick buck or a nostalgic holding on to something past. His words—and Schrader's images—draw out a sense of obligation that, with his father's death and Wade's disappearance, binds him to this place like a memory or history. The ending also reinforces something that we have sensed all along: if the story in *Affliction* could be said to "belong" to any one person, it would be as much the property of Rolfe as it is of Wade. Perhaps everything we were told, everything that happened, has been Rolfe's attempt to claim ownership not of the property that comes to him with Wade's disappearance but ownership of the past, so that he can tell its story. These stories of brothers, fathers, and best friends—stories that, as Rolfe admits, we can never fully understand—demand to be retold, not only from character to character but, as we have seen, from film to film. It may be that this is what we are left with in *Affliction:* not the security of ownership but a cinematic milieu where the phantasms and stories of the past—the director's past as well as that of the characters—cover everything like a deep snow that refuses to thaw and melt away.

Prequels and Obsessive Loves: *Dominion* and *Forever Mine*

The final moments of *Affliction* provide a tempting point on which to conclude this study of Schrader's films. They affirm his status as a director who is able to explore difficult topics and characters while also engaging his audience on an emotional level. The Academy Award won by Coburn for his portrayal of Glen Whitehouse and Nolte's nomination for his portrayal of Wade add weight to this conclusion. Yet Schrader's production history since *Affliction* illustrates the difficulty of pinning his films down and the inherently unstable nature of his position within Hollywood. "*Affliction* was good in terms of reputation," Schrader observes. "It wasn't as good in terms of marketability. I didn't get one single offer. It didn't matter that the film was nominated for Academy Awards. I wasn't the filmmaker people wanted" (qtd. in Powers 30).

The offer to direct the prequel to *The Exorcist* (1973) came after Schrader's critical success with *Auto Focus*. It was the first time since *Cat People* that Schrader was given directorial control of a large-budget, studio-supported film. During the 1980s and 1990s, he was able to get around the problems associated with working in the risk-averse environment of Hollywood by making do with smaller and smaller budgets. As Schrader explains, the smaller the financial stakes, the greater the opportunity to explore challenging stories and characters:

There are story demands of a $40-plus million film that don't exist for a $7 million film. Even *Auto Focus,* I couldn't have told that story for $12 or $14 million. You've got to tell it for $6 or $7 million, otherwise you can't have that ending or that character, you've got to have something more conventional. But [*The Exorcist* prequel] kind of demands a conventional arc, and you know it has to have a positive ending, because Merrin's [Stellan Skarsgård] going to have to go on and be in *The Exorcist.* So our final shot is the final shot of *The Searchers*—Merrin walks out of the hospital, across the square, framed in the doorway, and he's obliterated by the dust-storm. (*SOS* 282)

Schrader's allusion to *The Searchers* reminds us of his background as part of the film-school generation of New Hollywood directors. For many of this generation, the final moments of Ford's film, where Ethan, framed in the doorway of the homestead, turns his back on the family and heads out into the wilderness, encapsulated not only the loneliness that accompanied Ethan's quest but also "the psychological instability of the pioneer" (*SOS* 155). It was this image of alienated masculinity that Schrader pushed to the limits of acceptability in films such as *Taxi Driver, Rolling Thunder,* and *Hardcore.* Schrader's return to this iconic moment at the end of *The Exorcist* prequel is apt, given that one of the films that marked the rise to power of his generation of American directors and set a pattern for its co-option by Hollywood was William Friedkin's *The Exorcist.* The commercial success achieved by Friedkin's film confirmed that Hollywood's commercial slump was over and set an important precedent for a type of large-budget, effects-driven cinema that dominated Hollywood filmmaking in the years to come (Cook, *Lost Illusions* 105). The film's use of controversial content, highly stylized atmospherics, and clever marketing provided an object lesson in how easily the novelty of the New Hollywood could be made to serve old Hollywood demands.

Viewed from this perspective, it should come as no surprise that, despite embarking on the production of the prequel fully aware of the aesthetic costs of working with a $40 million budget, Schrader's involvement with the film quickly soured. After presenting a rough cut to the head of Morgan Creek, the production company that owns the rights to the franchise, "creative differences" culminated in an announcement that Schrader had left the project. A new director, Renny Harlin, was hired, and over the next few months, a very different version of the film was constructed using a rewritten script, new actors in key supporting roles, and six weeks' worth of reshooting at Cinecitta Studios in Rome. This version was released in 2004 under the title *Exorcist: The Beginning*. Normally, this would have been the end of the story. In 2005, however, Morgan Creek allowed Schrader to complete his version of the film. The reason for their turnaround was the opportunity to recoup what had become a substantial investment by capitalizing on the shelved film's box-office and DVD potential. A version of the completed film was screened for the first time at the Brussels Fantasy Film Festival in March 2005. After receiving positive reviews in *Variety* and elsewhere, *Dominion: Prequel to the Exorcist* (2005), as Schrader's version came to be known, had its U.S. premiere on May 20, 2005.

Viewed side by side, the differences between the two films provide a useful glimpse into Schrader's approach to drama. As one would expect, Schrader's telling of the story is more concerned with the internal dilemmas faced by Father Merrin than in the visceral thrills of the horror genre. The demon that Merrin struggles with is both a supernatural force and a capacity for unspeakable evil that resides within all men. A terrible event during the war has stripped Merrin of his faith in God and the church. Unable to overcome this experience of evil, Merrin, like Ethan in *The Searchers*, becomes a wanderer moving from one archaeological dig to the next. These aspects of Merrin's character are present in the original script by Caleb Carr and William Wisher, but they gain weight through Schrader's framing of Merrin's predicament in terms of other characters and situations. Merrin is another light sleeper: someone who paces the floor struggling to make sense of experience and find a way forward. At the end of the film, Merrin makes peace with the church, not because he has reconciled himself to its problems or rediscovered a conviction once lost but because he has no alternative: "The church is a leaky structure, but it's all I have." After uttering these words, Merrin, like Ethan before him, turns his back on home and disappears into the dust storm.

By aligning Merrin's struggle to find meaning with Ethan's predicament at the end of *The Searchers*, Schrader invites us to read *Dominion* according to a larger narrative context of alienation and estrangement that has come to define his films. The final moments of *Dominion* also highlight that, as much as he is influenced by European cinematic forms and ideas, the traditions, genres, and iconography of American cinema provide the bedrock for Schrader's films. As a screenwriter and director, Schrader always has one eye on dark moments such as the final scene of *The Searchers* and one eye on the demands of the marketplace. Perhaps Schrader realized early on in his career that Ethan is less an outsider figure than a central part of a story that the American cinema tells over and over again. Recasting Ethan in this way means no longer thinking of Schrader as on the margins of Hollywood cinema but at the place where the familiar icons are broken down and reworked.

Taking up this suggestion leads to an engagement with films such as *Light Sleeper, Affliction,* and *Auto Focus* and also films that have fared less well in the marketplace. The most interesting example of this is *Forever Mine,* a film Schrader had been nurturing since 1989. When he finally got the chance to make the film, it was never released theatrically but sold directly to cable television. Even before these difficulties, Schrader regarded the film as a challenge. Shortly after its completion, he described it as "an old-fashioned romance of the highest order, a real melodrama, which I wrote and directed and financed. Nobody paid me to do this film. If a studio had made it, everyone would be saying that I had whored out, but in fact I had to fight to raise the financing, so if I did whore out, I whored out to my own melodramatic side" (Bliss 6).

Some years later, Schrader was still perplexed about the film: "I'm so torn about this film, because in a way I want it to be brainless romantic entertainment, but I'm not a brainless romantic person, so it's not what comes naturally to me. *Affliction* is what comes naturally to me—that is the simplest thing in the world, to make that work" (*SOS* 264). Schrader describes the film's story about two lovers who manage to reunite after many years as "a tribute to Douglas Sirk" (Bliss 6). In Sirk's melodramas of the 1950s, emotional entanglements find expression through a highly stylized approach to staging and design. *Forever Mine* takes from Sirk's films this attempt to channel emotion across every aspect of the screen. The sensuality of the relationship is matched by the sensuality of the film's design and cinematography. For the first time in many years, Schrader worked with the cinematographer John Bailey, who had shot *American Gigolo, Cat People, Mishima,* and *Light of Day.* Bailey's elegant tracking shots and use of warm, pastel colors in the opening half of the film create a sense of the story's otherworldliness. Turning back to look at the luxury hotel that serves as the film's primary setting, Ella Brice (Gretchen Mol) sums up a feeling shared by many in the audience: "It looks like a fantasy castle . . . and this is a fantasy land."

Forever Mine's creation of a fairytale setting is not meant to undercut the story. Rather, it highlights something specific about the way this story is told. Right from the opening shot of the hotel framed against a bright blue sky that fades to night, everything we see in *Forever Mine* is reflected through the prism of the relationship or, more precisely, the memory of the relationship that Alan Riply (Joseph Fiennes) and Ella nurture. This is why Schrader leaves out moments of explication concerning the characters and the nature of their mutual attraction. Rather than exploring the psychological context of the relationship, Schrader's focus is on the mark it leaves on the characters and the film itself. In this sense, *Forever Mine* represents not a break from Schrader's earlier films but a recasting of familiar themes of obsession, memory, and yearning in the guise of an old-fashioned love story.

During the first half of the film, it is clearly Alan's memory that provides the vehicle for the narrative. We first encounter Alan at the

Forever Mine: Alan (Joseph Fiennes) and Ella (Gretchen Mol) rendezvous at the beach where she is on holiday with her husband.

end of a slow track along the aisle of a plane. At this point in the film, Alan is known by a different name: Manuel Esquema. His facial disfigurement and reserve immediately set him apart from his traveling companion, Javier Cesti (Vincent Laresca). When the flight attendant asks Señor Esquema if New York is his final destination, he simply nods and looks straight ahead—as if his mind is somewhere else. Where his mind is, in fact, is fourteen years earlier. This is revealed by a cross-fade that substitutes Esquema's disfigured face with a younger, unblemished version of the same face. This, we learn, is the face of Alan Riply. In the next few moments, everything that happens—Alan's arrival at the luxury hotel, his bantering with Javier and the other cabana boys, the camera's tracking of the two friends out of the locker room, through the grounds of the hotel, and down to the beach—is preparation for the first encounter between the two lovers. The significance of this event is conveyed by the way, all at once, the sound of Javier's voice fades and a slow-motion zoom reveals Alan looking intently at something offscreen. The film then cuts to a shot of the ocean. A second or two later, Ella rises out of the ocean dressed in a white bathing suit.

The zoom into Alan's face, the use of slow motion, the fading out of surrounding sounds: all these techniques follow a familiar stylistic schema replayed and even parodied across countless Hollywood films. *Forever Mine* departs from what we have seen many times before in its introduction of a subtle sense of disturbance. This disturbance is suggested by the way the shot of Ella rising out of the ocean is too close to Ella to approximate Alan's point of view. Strange, too, is the way the shot of Alan looking intently towards the ocean *anticipates* Ella's appearance. (Later, Alan will write in one of his prison letters to Ella: "The sight of your body affects me so strongly, has always affected me so strongly, that I believe I was born to see it.") Instead of a smooth unfolding of shots joined in a successive time frame, we are presented with a kind of stutter whereby an event happens and then happens again.

Schrader's staging of Ella's first appearance emphasizes the primal nature of the encounter and its status as memory-work: an intensified rendition of something viewed in retrospect over and over again. That it is not only Alan but also Ella caught in the grips of memory is suggested by the lines from Gustave Flaubert's *Madame Bovary* that we later hear her reading to the nursing-home residents: "Little by little, the faces became confused in her memory. . . . Some of the details vanished, but the longing remained." Just as neither Alan nor Ella can distance themselves from the memory of their relationship, the film also refuses to leave behind the memory of other characters caught in the grips of emotions and attachments they can't leave behind—we might think here of LeTour from *Light Sleeper* or even Wade from *Affliction*. But an equally appropriate precedent for the film's portrait of obsession is Mishima. The opening shot of the hotel that over the course of the credits changes from bright sunlight to full night echoes the opening shot of *Mishima* that records the rising of the sun out of the ocean. Both films begin with an image that burns itself into the film. The moment that most directly connects the two films involves the exchange of looks between Mishima as a young boy and the Onnagata in the theater. As in the presentation of Ella's first appearance, the filming of the Onnagata's languid gesture of raising the cigarette to his mouth evokes a sense of rapture, of being overwhelmed by a person or feeling, and how this stays in one's memory, gathering force.

Something else calls *Mishima* to mind: not only the way both films draw out an intensification of experience through a highly stylized use of color, costume, setting, and design but also the way the characters seem driven to stage and narrate their own story. "My need to transform reality," pronounces the troubled Japanese author, "was an urgent necessity, as important as three meals a day or sleep." This principle is given formal expression through the interplay of dramatized portions of Mishima's fictional writings and the film's presentation of biographical incidents. In *Forever Mine,* the effort of transforming reality is part and parcel of Alan's single-minded attachment to Ella. After spending the night with Ella, Alan takes her to a beachside bar and restaurant. "What's your story?" he asks. When Ella coyly replies, "It's not very interesting," Alan responds: "Then . . . let's make a new story. I Am Born: The Story of Alan and Ella. We open on a beachfront bar. Let's pretend it's called . . . The Seabreeze. . . . They've come in from the ocean. He's just a cabana boy, but he has dreams."

Alan's story refuses to recognize the conditions limiting its fulfillment. "Everybody has a purpose," he tells Ella's husband, Mark Brice (Ray Liotta): "It is my purpose to be with Ella. Nothing can change that. Not you. Not the police. Not the courts. It's just a fact." When Ella works up the courage to tell her story, the story she tells is halting in delivery and grounded in everyday realities: "Okay, here's my story: I was in the secretarial pool . . . Xeroxing, getting coffee. . . . Guys making . . . guys making jokes about me, the way I dressed. . . . I didn't have any money. We didn't have any money. We moved from place to place. And then, guess what? The boss started asking me out." The other story surrounding the two lovers comes from Mark: "There's two types of people in this world," he warns Alan. "Assholes and pricks. You're an asshole, and I'm a prick." The presence of these different stories creates a drama based on competing scenarios battling to dominate or have the final word. And for some time, Schrader keeps them running simultaneously, as if he is not sure which of these various stories and storytellers should dominate or have the final word: the obsessed lover, the woman trying to keep her feet on the ground, or the corrupt politician.

After Alan is shot in the face and left for dead, the romantic principles of the first half of the film give way to a more familiar story of violence, revenge, and shady deals. The languorous pacing and elegant camera moves are replaced by a more rapid style of cutting and pacing. And instead of the sultry pop songs that accompanied the young lovers, the introduction of Michael Been's voice conjures the same heavy sense of predetermined outcomes that Schrader employed in *Light Sleeper.* There is something inevitable about the final confrontation, when Mark catches up with Alan and Ella. His final declaration to Alan—"We are all going to die for love. I'm a romantic too"—represents one more recasting of the film's story. But Schrader does not allow this to stand as the final word. Instead, the film ends in the back of an ambulance with Ella urging Alan to think back and remember Key Biscayne and remember their love story. As Alan drifts in and out of consciousness, the final seconds reprise moments from earlier in the film. On the soundtrack, Alan and Ella take turns telling the story of their love: "I realized nothing would be the same. I realized my life had changed. . . . I realized that it would be important. I realized you would be forever mine."

"Give All to Love"

Schrader's films are about the act of telling stories as a cinematic process and a function of identity. This is evident in the way the stories told in his films consciously allude to and rework stories that have been told before—for example, *The Searchers, Vertigo,* and *The Conformist.* It is also evident in the way storytelling itself has a direct bearing on the fate of the characters. In *Taxi Driver,* Travis's habit of keeping a journal consciously evokes the plight of the young priest in Bresson's *Diary of a Country Priest.* But it also alerts us to the central place of writing and telling a story—about oneself and others—in Travis's struggle. In *Mishima* and *Patty Hearst,* the problem for the central characters and indeed the films themselves is to find a way of telling a story in which the notion of a fixed and stable identity is either no longer operative or, in Patty's case, brutally undermined. As Schrader's career developed, the abiding interest in storytelling became bound up in a fascination with the possibility of finding ourselves implicated in stories that seem to tell us. The interlocking couples in *The Comfort of Strangers;* LeTour's inability to look forward; the story of male violence that swallows up Wade and Rolfe in *Affliction:* at the heart of each of these scenarios is the disturbing sense of having one's story told ahead of time and always being too late to effect change. Perhaps Schrader's most significant contribution to the tradition of American cinematic storytelling is the development of such temporally enfolded narratives and characters.

At the end of *Forever Mine,* we are not sure if Alan will survive the shooting. It is not that Schrader can't decide about the relationship; it is rather that the differences and tensions at the heart of the film's competing stories—Alan's, Ella's, and Mark's—refuse reconciliation or easy solution. This is why the final scene that spells out the fate of the couple is withheld. In place of the grace notes that conclude films like *American Gigolo* and *Light Sleeper,* Schrader leaves it up to the audience to fill in their own conclusion to a story whose own investments are abundantly clear. "Give All to Love" is the title of a famous love poem by Ralph Waldo Emerson; it is also the slogan painted on the wall of Alan's dingy hotel room in New York. Alan's room reminds us of all the other rooms occupied by Schrader's existential heroes: Mishima, Travis, Julian, LeTour—even Patty in her closet. *Forever Mine* recasts the monomania and isolation housed in these spaces through an engagement with romantic love.

Something larger than the purity of Alan's emotion is at stake here. Alan's attachment to Ella bears the marks of the kind of obsessive behavior we have come to expect of Schrader's characters; but it lacks the violent aspect that, in the other films, keeps us at a distance. *Forever Mine* warns against positioning Schrader's films in opposition to Hollywood or reading them solely in terms of male violence. It illustrates Schrader's capacity to pursue a distinct set of figures and themes across a range of different genres, narrative styles, and collaborative engagements. That Schrader was able to switch so quickly from the gloom of *Affliction* to *Forever Mine*'s embrace of emotion and then take on the strangely dissociated sexual antics in *Auto Focus* illustrates the difficulty of pinning his films down to a single style. Some time ago, Schrader offered his own provisional summation of the nature and direction of his work: "Perhaps my 'style' will be a permanent and contradictory tension. Perhaps it is moving toward a harmony as yet unknown to me. Perhaps it will lose even the value of this tension" (qtd. in Nichols 13). Halfway through the fourth decade of Schrader's working life, this permanent and contradictory tension may not produce films that are settled or easy to place; but what it continues to provide is a vital reworking of the defining tropes and archetypes of the American cinema.

Notes

1. Although Schrader did not complete this study, he published an extended essay on the topic. See Schrader, "Canon Fodder."

2. Elsaesser's "The Pathos of Failure" was originally published in *Monogram* 6 (1975): 13–19. It has been reprinted in *The Last Great American Picture Show;* page numbers refer to this reprint.

3. Hereafter this text will be abbreviated in parenthetical references as *SOS*.

4. I have transcribed passages of dialogue and voiceover comments as they are spoken in the films rather than as they appear in the published screenplays. Those familiar with Schrader's published screenplays will notice minor variations.

5. See, for example, the essays on *American Gigolo* by Peter Lehman, William Luhr, and Robert T. Eberwein in Ruppert, *Gender.*

6. For an account of how the film blends information and events drawn from Mishima's memoirs, autobiographically inspired fictions, and published biographies, see Wilson.

7. For Schrader's description of the history of Springsteen's connection to the film, see *SOS* (184).

8. Patty's voiceover shares characteristics with that of Sunny von Bulow (Glenn Close) in Barbet Schroeder's *Reversal of Fortune* (1990). The fact that Nicholas Kazan authored both scripts highlights the importance of his contribution to *Patty Hearst*'s overall design.

9. Stephen Prince provides a useful overview of the distribution difficulties faced by independent filmmakers in the 1980s: "In 1986 and 1987, 382 independent films failed to receive distribution. Approximately 25 percent of these unreleased titles went directly to video. For such films, lacking stars and glitz production values, video could be an instant graveyard" (Prince 121).

10. This reading of Robert's story is put forward by Combs (Review of *Cortesie* 6).

Interview with Paul Schrader |

This interview was conducted on September 19 and 20, 2005, in New York City.

GEORGE KOUVAROS: Now that *Dominion* has been released, what other projects are you currently working on?

PAUL SCHRADER: Well, I've agreed to direct a film called *Adam Resurrected* from a very famous Israeli novel by Yoram Kaniuk. It's being rewritten now. We hope to shoot next July: Israel, Romania, and maybe Germany. It's a very serious film, a very heavy film. And a terrific book. I like the script a lot. The script is being rewritten now. I'm working with the writer.

For years and years, I've been trying to do a film called *The Walker* and, strangely enough, I have it financed, but now I don't have an actor. The window to do it is closing or will probably close in two weeks. So that's sort of happening, I mean that could happen very quickly, and suddenly I'd be squeezing that in before *Adam Resurrected,* but I don't know.

GK: *The Walker* is a script that you've spoken about on a number of occasions.

PS: Yeah, I know, I know. I've really come to regret it. It's so hard to always explain why a thing doesn't happen. I've been to bat with four different actors on that, and I've lost all four. . . . I could give you a copy of the script. Maybe you want to talk about it after having a read of the script.

GK: Sure, but could I ask you now about its relationship to the trilogy involving *Taxi Driver, American Gigolo,* and *Light Sleeper?*

PS: Well, I'm hoping that the trilogy will become a tetralogy. That's the idea of it. *Light Sleeper* bookends *Taxi Driver,* and *The Walker* will bookend *American Gigolo.* That's the idea of it, but we'll see. . . .

GK: It seems as if what you are doing with these films and characters is exploring your own feelings about a certain phase of life and how your responses to things change over time.

PS: Well, you have a central character whom I've described as The Peeper, The Wanderer, The Voyeur, The Loner that comes out of your character and comes out of the boy I was going from Grand Rapids to Los Angeles, coming from a rather strict background and then being confronted with L.A. circa 1968. And that sense of the push-pull, the sense that you can't stop looking, but you can't get inside the room either. So, you're frozen there against the window and passing judgment. Then, as you grow older, that sense evolves and it goes through phases: anger, narcissism, or anxiety. Now the fourth phase I want to deal with is superficiality: pretending that life has no meaning.

GK: Is this in some ways a return to the environment of *American Gigolo?*

PS: Absolutely. It's the same way that *Light Sleeper* is a return to the *Taxi Driver* environment, New York City. *Taxi Driver* is in the front seat; *Light Sleeper* is in the back seat.

GK: There's the key difference. What would be the difference between the superficiality of *American Gigolo* and what we find in *The Walker?*

PS: The character knows that he's superficial and, in fact, prides himself on it. He has made it part of his protection. I think the gigolo role was, in many ways, really just a thin guy. *The Walker* is much more complex.

GK: But even the thin guy in *American Gigolo* underwent a transformation at the end.

PS: Yeah, but I'm not quite sure how authentic it was. Part of me thinks I just stapled it onto him; you know, took it from Bresson and stapled it on. If I had to do it over again, I'm not sure whether that was an authentic transition or one that was simply imposed on him by his maker.

GK: But you still believe that transformation has to happen in your work?

PS: Yes, some kind.

GK: When you wrote about Bresson, you identified it as a central part of his work: at the end of a film, there has to be an opening up of the character to a dimension of the spirit and the supernatural.

PS: As we get older—particularly as the whole process of movies and film storytelling gets older—people have different notions of what's necessary dramatically. They start to see a lot of the melodramatic machinery of the past as outdated. Reality television isn't popular for no reason. It's popular because we're tiring of artificial drama, and reality TV seems less artificial.

GK: But it also conforms to quite traditional narrative and character arcs. The process of transformation that drives your work seems to be something quite different. I don't know if you could call it melodramatic, but it does seem to be an attempt to represent change—a change in someone's sense of who they are.

PS: Like everyone else, I'm becoming less and less interested in the heavy machinery of movies that strike me as being a remnant of the nineteenth century. But that's a whole other subject, one I've been thinking about a lot and trying to write about.

GK: This is something that you've spoken about before: the idea that cinema is at a point of change where the kinds of characters that interest you, the existential characters, no longer have a place.

PS: Well, I think the point of change is even greater than I thought before. I've been doing a fair amount of research because I agreed to write this book for Faber on the film canon, and I found myself thrown into all this work about the history of the notion of the canon and why it went out of fashion. Film itself, in fact, is one of the things that destroyed the notion of the canon. When people talk about a film canon, it's kind of a contradictory phrase. So, how can you have a film canon? I've been thinking about that. While I was writing this morning, I was thinking about an argument put forward by Dudley Andrew concerning the transitional nature of cinema.[1] It comes from a seed idea by Walter Benjamin. Andrew's contention is that motion pictures are a way station in the cavalcade of art history, a stopover en route from nineteenth-century written narrative to the twenty-first-century world of synthetic images and sounds. While this is perhaps a little bit extreme, it's also very much to the point.

GK: One thing that cinema did, certainly, back in the sixties was to make a canon out of things that were considered noncanonical.

PS: Yep, the Andrew Sarris thing.

GK: Then we had a period where the canon lost its value, and film came to be treated as just another cultural text to be analyzed. Among film writers, things are changing again. There is now a sense that we need to be able to recognize, discuss, and try to teach what constitutes the landmarks of cinema.

PS: That's the whole point of what I'm working on now in this long introductory essay. There's a de facto canon in populist literature, and there's a de facto canon in the academy. So, if you have a de facto canon, why not try to find a way to justify it and raise the bar so fucking high that only a few films get over it?

GK: So, the de facto canon lives?

PS: Yeah, I mean, since it exists anyway. We've now reached that point in film history where, without a canon, you cannot talk about history. When I was starting out, there were still people who had seen virtually everything. There's now so much out there that it beggars the imagination. Film students today have to specialize. You can't be a film authority in a way that you could be thirty years ago. There's just too much. [Laughs.]

GK: To specialize one needs to first get a sense of the films that constitute the general field.

PS: That's right, the canon. So, you can look at the high points of Japanese cinema and Iranian cinema and screwball comedy and ask, "What interests me?"

GK: You said that the canon would be quite an exclusive group. What criteria would you use to define the qualities of a canonical film?

PS: That's what I've been working on now. I've been working on this for almost a year and taking classes at Columbia. I'm up to that point in the introductory essay where I've gone through the history of the notion of the canon and the history of aesthetics in terms of the creation of the canon and why the canon collapsed. And now I'm in the section of the essay where I'm trying to say under what conditions can there still be a canon. The first condition is that you have to understand cinema as a transitional art in that it's the art form of the twentieth century, and it's maybe all over already. You have to look at films in the context of where they came from and where they're going, somewhere between Victorian melodrama and Andy Warhol rethinking the static shot.

GK: Given your own history as a critic, what role do you see for the critic in defining the canon? For the canon to exist, it needs people to invest in it and sustain it through a practice of critical writing that is quite different to the kinds of critical writing that we confront on a day-to-day basis. Where this comes from is reading some of your comments about criticism as a cadaverous activity in that it deals with something that isn't alive. When I read that, I thought immediately about the role of the critic in animating a film, a painting, or piece of music. It seems to me that if one sets out to revive the notion of the canon—whether it is in film or any other medium—one is also setting out to revive a form of critical writing capable of bringing the work to life for a reader.

PS: The book was presented to me initially as a variant of Harold Bloom's *The Western Canon.* Bloom starts off by asking: If you have a canon, what author must be included? If it's literature, it must be Shakespeare. How can you have a canon without Shakespeare? And if you have Shakespeare, what work? You must have *Hamlet;* otherwise you don't have Shakespeare. So, let's look at *Hamlet* and say, What makes it canonical? And then you start to work from there. That's a very clever argument. For me, the key film would be *Rules of the Game* [1939]. You can't have a canon without [Jean] Renoir, and you can't have Renoir without *Rules of the Game.* So, the question becomes: What makes *Rules of the Game* canonical? [Laughs.] But I'm not that far yet. I'm still talking about the history of the notion of the canon. I'm not even into specific works.

GK: It reminds me somewhat of the opening scene in *Hardcore* where the elders are gathered in the room on Christmas morning debating the theological significance of passages from the Bible. This type of endeavor still seems very important to you.

PS: Well, when it comes to Protestants, people get confused between the evangelicals and the fundamentalists and so forth. There are basically two kinds of Protestants: there's faith-based and doctrine-based. Mostly, when people think of evangelicals they are thinking of faith-based people. And that's just: "I believe . . . and there's nothing to talk about because I believe. God and Jesus told me and I know." Doctrine-based people are people who argue their way through. So, a lot of my upbringing in the church was really just argumentation . . . a lot of catechism, a lot of intellectual debate. There is such a large part of Christianity that is antiintellectual. And the moment you start talking about Christianity, people assume that you're part of the antiintellectual group, the anti-Darwin, antiscience group. And God knows, there are plenty of those. But that wasn't my background at all.

GK: Have you got to the stage where you have an idea of who you would put into that canon apart from Renoir's *Rules of the Game*?

PS: I have a rough idea: a lot of Frenchmen. But because of the nature of film, I don't know if it's necessarily auteur driven. It's important to understand that there are great collaborative films. *The Third Man* [1949] is a great collaborative film. And maybe it's as great a film as a film that has a much stronger sense of authorship.

GK: I'd like to ask about the idea of collaboration. One of the things that defines your career is the way that it has developed through strong collaborations, for example, with Scorsese on *Taxi Driver*, with Scarfiotti on *American Gigolo* and *Cat People*, then an important collaboration with Pinter on *The Comfort of Strangers*. How did these collaborations change your approach to cinema?

PS: Well, it's always fun to come up against a strong set of ideas or themes. I think the reason *Affliction* is good is because Russell Banks is really strong. Now, Russell was not an overt collaborator, but he was definitely a collaborator on *Affliction*. If you're writer and director both, sometimes you get lost doing both jobs. As I've said before, the writer and director—they lie to each other. And you often don't realize until you edit the extent to which you have believed your own lies.

Right now, I'm working with Noah Stollman on *Adam Resurrected*. We have a terrific book. There's a good script, and we're trying to make it better. He keeps saying stuff to me, and I said to him, "Don't bullshit me. I'm a writer too. I know that stuff you're saying. You're whistling in the dark. You're trying to convince me that something is working when it's not working. I've done it a hundred times myself. Let's go back and try to make it work." Well, I can recognize that when he's saying it to me. I often don't recognize it when I'm saying it to myself. [Laughs.]

GK: Watching *Dominion,* there were two moments that, for me, seemed to really shout Paul Schrader. One was the *Light Sleeper* moment: the overhead shot of Merrin on the bed where he . . .

PS: Going in to that period dream sequence . . .

GK: Yes, and there's a series of cross-fades of Merrin occupying different positions on the bed, very similar to the way Dafoe is shown in *Light Sleeper.* The other moment, of course, is the final shot that reprises the final shot of *The Searchers.*

PS: Those are visual things, but also the two religious discussions between the younger and the older priests. Those were in the original script. I rewrote them, and they got better. But I think another director would have bailed on those. One of the things that attracted me to the script was the fact that those conversations were in there. I didn't realize at the time that they really didn't want that movie. I assumed because I was being asked to direct it and was ready to go that they actually wanted that script. [Laughs.]

GK: Again, it's another thing that defines your work: your willingness to stick your neck out and do those kinds of scenes.

PS: *Adam Resurrected* is a very, very ambitious book. It was written in 1971. It's the kind of book they don't really write anymore. It was written at the time of things like *Slaughterhouse Five, Sophie's Choice,* and *Enemies: A Love Story.* It's about a psychiatric clinic for camp survivors in Israel. It's very heavy. The main character survived the war by becoming a dog for the commandant. The Israelis who are financing it had given it to Barry Levinson and Sydney Pollack, and both Barry and Sydney said, "How can you do this? How do you make this film?" So, Ehud [Bleiberg], the producer, was talking to an agent at ICM [International Creative Management] and said: "Well, what directors do you represent who'll do anything, who have no fear?" And up came my name. "Schrader will do anything." And that's how I got asked—because I'm certainly not Jewish, I'm not Israeli. It was the same thing with *Patty*

Hearst and, to some degree, with *Auto Focus:* How do you do that? How do you make it work?

I remember I had a conversation once with Sydney Pollack. Sydney was talking about directors such as myself who come into his office—Mirage Productions—trying to get his help to get a film made. And he said, "These young independent filmmakers, I look at them, and I don't see much difference between us. I don't see how they're really any different to me." I said: "Well Sydney, I've made two films that I knew by the time I started filming had no financial chance whatsoever. But, in both cases, I thought they were interesting films and would be worth the effort to make. So, would you ever do that?" He thought for a while and asked: "If I knew a film was going to fail financially?" I said: "Yeah." "No, I wouldn't make it." He said: "I would back out if it became clear it would fail." I knew *Mishima* had no financial future, and I knew *Patty Hearst* could never really be successful. But they seemed worth making.

GK: Taking those sorts of risks also takes an enormous physical and emotional toll. And then, after the film is made, getting a distributor . . .

PS: I would beg to differ. I think the opposite is much more exhausting—making a piece of shit. Talk about a toll. I don't know how they do it. I don't know how those people go out and make that same movie they've seen a hundred times and that somebody else has made a hundred times. Going to the factory in order to stamp out the same object you've been stamping out all your life. How do you do that in the arts? I mean, that would drive me crazy. Going out and saying, "How the hell am I going to pull this off?"—that keeps you awake; that makes you excited and makes you alive. So, I just don't really know how directors do it just as a job. I think everything has to be a matter of, "I don't know if you can do this." We may be having dinner in a few years, and I'll say to you: "You know that movie I didn't know if I could pull off? Well, I was right; you can't pull that one off. But I had to make it to find out."

GK: It seems to me that all of your films pose the question: "How do I make this film?" Or, more correctly, "How do I tell this story?" "How do I tell a story about a character as unaware as Bob Crane or as contradictory as Mishima?"

PS: That's why I respect a director like Kubrick more than, say,

Hitchcock or Ford. I'm not saying that Kubrick is a better director, but I respect him more because with Kubrick it was always, "How am I going to solve this problem?" *Dr. Strangelove* [1964], that's a solution. *Barry Lyndon* [1975], well that's a different solution. So too is *Clockwork Orange* [1971] . . . *The Shining* [1980]. You're always grappling with the material to see who will win.

GK: Is this what you meant in your interviews with Jackson when you described the importance of seeing the film? You were talking about the production of *American Gigolo* and how it was the first time you had a clear sense of how to visualize the story.

PS: No, what I was talking about there is the difference between visual logic and illustration. Most filmmaking is just illustration. For example, a script says: "Man asleep in his room." You get a bed, you get a room, you put in a man asleep, and you shoot it. There you go: "Man asleep in his room." You're just illustrating the story. At some point, you start to see it; you start to see the images. I am not that kind of filmmaker. I'm still, by and large, an illustrator as a filmmaker. But now I have come to the point where I start to see it somewhat. I'm not like Nic Roeg, who lived in a kind of nonverbal world of images. It's about the transition when you start to see images as ideas.

GK: Could this be one of the criteria for the canon, then, that an image is not just an illustration but that it approximates the thing in itself?

PS: That's what Walter Benjamin's talking about when he talks about photography freeing the image from the tyranny of the writer. But you can only talk about film in terms of multiple criteria because it is such a mixed media. Some films are best evaluated as writing; some films are best evaluated as images; some in terms of other factors. You really have to have a sliding scale of multiple criteria to evaluate film. And that's where it gets so tricky. Some films you really want an architectural critic to write the article, and sometimes you want a poet to write the article.

GK: When you started filmmaking, you had a clear sense of who your touchstones were in terms of other filmmakers. When you mentioned architecture before, I immediately thought of Antonioni's influence on films like *American Gigolo* and *Light Sleeper.* You've also spoken about the influence of Bertolucci and classical auteurs like Ford, Sirk, and Hitchcock. Do you still see these directors as valuable touchstones on your current projects?

PS: Well, you find yourself referencing them in some way. On *Dominion,* I went on a research trip to the Turkana district in Kenya where the film is set—even though we didn't shoot it there. I was right by the Sudanese border. It's pretty wild country. And once I got out there, it really struck me like the American West. And that's where all the Western imagery started coming from. All of a sudden, I realized the script is like *Shane,* and the images are like Ford. It's not that you say, "I'm going to make a film like John Ford," but you look at the problem, and as you think about the problem you say, "Wow, this is really like a Western." The question then is: "Which Western is it like?" It comes in that way; it doesn't come in the other way. It comes in after you've defined the problem. So, if you've defined the problem of one of alienation, then, of course, you're going to scoot back to Antonioni and look at those films. If you've defined the problem as one of one of sexual obsession, you're going to look at different films.

GK: In a way, the canon is also part of the problem-solving strategy that you've talked about in terms of Eames's work. The canonical film can be seen as a way to think about and visualize a relationship to the world, whether it's Crane's relationship to the world or whether it's LeTour's relationship to the world. The canon presents relationships, perhaps.

PS: Fortunately, whatever problem you're dealing with, there are laundry lists of films or books or paintings that have dealt with the same thing, and you need to reference those.

GK: Do you ever find that the laundry list can, at times, be suffocating?

PS: Well, there is that desire in the arts to burn down the academy and to kill your father. In some ways, the best example of this is *Jules and Jim* [1961], where it's shaking up all kinds of notions of storytelling. A lot of interesting filmmaking is just breaking the rules. [Jean-Luc] Godard once said: "People thought we had a style. But, for the most part, we were doing what they said we couldn't do. If they said you couldn't shoot a close-up with a wide angle, we'd shoot a close-up with a wide angle. If they said, you couldn't do a tracking shot hand-held; well we did a tracking shot hand-held." And, so, part of the so-called style was just the arbitrary perversity of breaking the rules.

GK: The problem was that, by the end of the seventies, Godard reached a point where he had no more rules to break. So he either had to reinvent the rules or find practices where there were rules that he could work against. Hence, he turns to painting in *Passion* [1982].

PS: It's amazing. There really are no rules now. There used to be a lot of rules. You can do anything in a movie now. And it's very hard to throw a viewer, very hard. These kids who have been raised on multichannel TV and video games, well, you can't throw them. You can juxtapose almost anything: different film stocks and mismatches and time sequences, and they'll just sit there and watch it. [Laughs.] And they'll put it together. Audiovisual literacy is so much more advanced for my children's generation than it was for mine.

GK: Do you think that's true in terms of issues like duration? Nothing can throw this generation . . . except time, except having to deal with a narrative that takes its time.

PS: Yeah.

GK: This is particularly relevant in the case of a film like *Affliction* that is all about the weight of time, the weight of the past. In *Light Sleeper,* as well, there's a strong interest in how people deal with time.

PS: You have to figure out a way to slow the audience's metabolism down. I mean, look at the credit sequence of *Affliction,* that's all it is: slow down. And you have to find a way, once they get in the theater, to keep them interested and let them know they can relax and just sit back. One of the things I loved about [Ingmar] Bergman's *Saraband* [2003] was just the hauteur of the film. The way it starts: it says basically, "I'm a serious person and this is a serious movie, and if you're not a serious viewer, you can get the fuck out now because this movie's not for you." [Laughs.] No pretense toward anything else.

GK: Another way that time works in your films is by returning to characters. In *Light Sleeper,* for example, time is a key theme—something the character is trying to deal with. But it's also something that operates on a broader level in terms of our sense of the film's connection to other films and characters, namely, *American Gigolo* and *Taxi Driver.* And with *The Walker,* as well, one can't help but sense that this character has an age or history that may be outside the immediate story but floating somewhere in the background.

PS: That's the hope, yeah. That's the hope.

GK: I want to ask you about *Forever Mine* as well. This is probably the film of yours that is the most underrated.

PS: Maybe I shouldn't have made it. Maybe I waited too long. It was a long time between when I wrote it and when I made it. When I wrote it, I was very much that kind of obsessional, romantic young man. By the time I came to direct it, I wasn't that much anymore. So, it was a little bit away from me. But I always wanted to do it.

GK: In terms of the figure of the obsessional romantic, the film that *Forever Mine* reminded me of in terms of your career was *Mishima.* There is a line in *Mishima* that, when I saw *Forever Mine,* immediately came to mind: "My need to transform reality was an urgent necessity, as important as three meals a day or sleep." And it's the same with Alan. There is something about his obsession that wants to transforms things, that doesn't believe in the way things are and, instead, is convinced that things can change. *Forever Mine* goes back to *Mishima* but without the same investment in violence as a means for individual transformation. I don't know if you want to talk about this film because you've said in the past you prefer not to go back to your films once they are finished.

PS: Well, I'm trying to remember it as you're speaking. I know I wanted to make it pretty badly. And I had given up on ever making it, and then it came together. But, by the time I made it, it was so unhip; it was so uncool. *Forever Mine* was so old-fashioned passionate when it was made. At around the same time, Todd Haynes did *Far from Heaven* [2002]. And Todd's film was very contemporary and hip and deconstructivist, and mine was just too, you know. . . . The film I wanted to make should have been made ten years before. It had lost its historical slot.

GK: It's interesting that the historical slot for something like *Auto Focus* is much more consistent. Your chances of finding an audience for that type of strange detachment, contradiction, and cluelessness are always going to be much greater. Then you go to a character like Merrin in *Dominion,* and his agonies are going to be much riskier to do.

PS: Particularly since horror has not worked as a period film since the thirties and forties. Ever since the rebirth of the horror genre with *The Exorcist,* nearly every successful horror film has been contemporary. And *Dominion* was never really a horror film. I have to be careful because I get confused between my desire to see that film exist—my struggle to complete it—and how it exists. My cold assessment of the film: I don't think it should have been made. If I had known where it was going to take me, I certainly wouldn't have done it. I wouldn't do it again. It was not a journey worth taking. It wasn't my film. It wasn't my idea. Doing a prequel to *The Exorcist* wouldn't be something that I would come up with, an idea that I would argue, "That should be done."

GK: But it did offer you the opportunity to work with a $40 million budget.

PS: Oh yeah, yeah. . . . It was grand. It was great fun, and I think the film has some value. It will interest some people. And, of course, its real value now is going to be for film students to look at the two versions. [Laughs.]

GK: Did the experience of making the film and the ensuing struggle to get your version released clarify anything for you regarding what the next phase of your career should be about?

PS: Well, I don't have that many films left. As much as I want to work, I think that with the films I have left I should try to do only something of value. That's why I was really very pleased that *Adam Resurrected* came by. This is a substantial book, a substantial script. I would rather do something really small of some value than do what Marty Scorsese's doing. I don't see the fun in that.

Interview continued the following day.

GK: Thanks for the *Walker* script. I really enjoyed reading it. It put what you said yesterday into context, answered some questions, and opened up other questions. When I was reading it, I kept thinking of Kevin Kline. That's not going to happen, I take it.

PS: No. I had four actors originally: Steve Martin, and then I couldn't close the deal with Steve. And then I had Kevin, and then Kevin decided to do Cole Porter [*De-Lovely;* 2004]—which is the same character. And then I had Tim Robbins—that was last year. Tim didn't want to go to Berlin, which is where I had it set up. And then I had Michael Keaton, who just dropped out six weeks ago without explanation. When I say I had these people, that means they've agreed to do it, one-on-one, orally. But no money has changed hands. Nothing has been signed. So, then, you get to the next step and you say, "Okay, you know, here's the deal, here's the start date." And then, things happen. . . . But I have the money, and I talked to the producer yesterday. He said, "Let's go into preproduction by the end of October and we'll make it with somebody."[2] [Laughs.]

GK: Was Dafoe interested?

PS: This character's funny. He's suave. He's funny. It's not Willem. I could get Willem to do it in a second. It's just not Willem. This is a social butterfly. Willem is not a social butterfly. And Gere is not funny. This is someone who hides himself by being funny. If the gigolo hides himself by being physically beautiful, the walker hides himself by being funny. I shouldn't be talking about this because it's been so frustrating for so long, and I swore I wouldn't talk about it anymore until I knew it was getting made.

GK: I did have questions about the script in terms of its relationship to the rest of your work. Do you mind if I ask you those questions?

PS: That's no problem.

GK: Around the time it was released, you described *Light Sleeper* as a response to your own sense of encroaching nostalgia, and falling prey to the temptation of thinking it was better before. This script seems to be about the temptations of an encroaching superficiality, a sense that now . . .

PS: Nothing really matters.

GK: *The Walker* seems to be about the dangers of growing old gracefully. And for the central character, for Carter Page, this means shutting himself off from personal commitment or engagement with the political realities around him. Do you think that's a fair summation?

PS: Yeah, it's a comment not only on my age but on the age we live in. You know, this sort of disengaged times where it's getting harder and harder to rouse people, to ignite them because the level of public cynicism is just so, so high.

GK: In the script there's a direct response to the standard justification for disengagement, namely, that no matter who you vote for or who gets elected, nothing really is going to change. What this script shows is how much things have changed and that, clearly, we are in a different and much harder time. . . . I was quite struck by how direct the script is in terms of its addressing of these sorts of issues.

PS: It does a bit, but it's not really a political document. Certainly, there are a lot of very pointed, political films around now. This stays within the bounds of a character study.

GK: In the past, you said that, in terms of your own work and career, it's important to be energized by a sense of opposition—"The day *that* stops being your cup of coffee, the game is over."[3] Is this still the case? Is the need to provide a voice of opposition still the thing that drives you to decide on a particular project?

PS: There's always been something adversarial and evangelical about my interest in film. It really began that way as a kid. Being interested in film was a measure of revolt. It was a measure of confronting the status quo, the machinery of the community you lived in. It doesn't seem like much of a revolt in today's eyes, but it was back then. . . . And my love of film, even before it was a love of film, was probably a love of trouble-making first. The films I fell in love with were troublemaking films. We showed *Viridiana* [dir. Luis Buñuel; 1961] on campus. What is this film but an act of aggression? It's pretty undisguised.

GK: Do you think films still offer young people that?

PS: No, no. In fact, precious little does. You know, which is unfortunate. . . .

GK: Music perhaps, which was also something that you were very interested in.

PS: There are so few rules left. I mean, it's getting harder and harder to break the rules. You really almost have to self-destruct to break the rules. Certainly, all the sort of traditional things like sex or deportment or language are pretty hard to get to offend much of anybody anymore.

GK: If you see that it becomes harder and harder to break the rules, then the other way to look at it is: What should we maintain? What should we treasure? What should we value? Which gets us back to the question of the canon.

PS: In the end, you have to believe in the same thing all humanists have believed in and religions have believed in, which is basically a variant on the Golden Rule: Love thy neighbor as thyself.

GK: This leads us to the issue of community in your films. Right from *Blue Collar* and *Hardcore,* you seem to be interested in linking your dramas to very specific community settings. More recently, a film like *Affliction* develops a strong sense of community complete with all its traumas and dark histories. In *Light Sleeper,* I was fascinated by the way you created a sense of community out of the remnants of New Age spirituality, the trade in white drugs and a failed counterculture moment.

It seems to me that, as much as all these films are character studies, they are also concerned with looking at where and how communities form—even if they're not the traditional ones.

PS: In *The Walker* it's the canasta game: Carter Page and his ladies. They form this little black-sheep community that sort of collapses.

The Walker: The canasta group: Chrissie (Mary Beth Hurt), Lynn (Kristin Scott Thomas), Natalie (Lauren Bacall), Car (Woody Harrelson), and Abigail (Lily Tomlin).

GK: And it's a community that, at first glance, can transcend political differences. You write at the start of the script: "It's not yet certain who is who, who is left, who is right, who is more or less powerful; one thing, however, is certain—they're having a heck of a good time." Then slowly you see that, in fact, it does matter. And if you think about the central character's place within this community, he, like a number of other characters, is something of an anachronism: he's from another, more genteel time. Yesterday, we spoke briefly about the various ways that time figures in your films. This might be another way: through the presence of characters who don't belong to their time or whose time has passed.

PS: Well, they are out of sync in some ways. . . . The thing that really makes a character interesting is when the character is working at cross-purposes. You know that wonderful phrase of Freud's: "The representation of a thing by its opposite." In other words, "I loved her so much I hit her." Whenever you're trying to make a character interesting, you're always looking at reverse behavior: the man that is so lonely that he does things that make him lonelier still; the person who is so desperate for love and community that he does the things that cut him off from those things. That makes for interesting characters. And it's also the heart and soul of self-examination. When you spend time on a couch or in a therapist's office, in the end it's going to come down to, "If I desire X, why do I do Y?" And that is the great mystery of every individual. And I think it makes interesting characters.

GK: What you love to explore, it seems, is not only the capacity for self-delusion and contradiction but also the capacity for characters to surprise themselves. I'm thinking here of the penultimate line in *The Walker*: "Strange how things work out," which is a slight variant of the line spoken by Ann in *Light Sleeper*: "Strange how things work." This line seems to capture the idea that we will never really know ourselves.

PS: Yeah, and it's a variant of the last line of *Pickpocket*: "What a strange road I've taken to come to you." In other words, I thought I was going in one direction, and all the time I was going in this direction.

GK: In the script, Page comes up with a classic piece of self-assessment: "I'm not naive, I'm superficial." For someone who is so sure of himself and so polished, it's quite a turnaround at the end of the film for him to admit: "It was what I wanted. I just didn't know it." In other words, he has taken himself by surprise.

PS: Sometimes, there's a kind of divine intervention in your life, and you have to sort of accept it or not. . . . When I came to New York, I was using drugs. I was still trying to effect reconciliation with the relationship I had screwed up in Los Angeles. And Mary Beth got pregnant. And she wanted to have a baby. My first response was panic. Meaning, that was the end of my old life. I would never get back with the girl in Los Angeles. I had to change. And then it occurred to me that this is what I really wanted to do, what I hadn't been able to do on my own. God had reached down and said, "Okay . . . I'll make it real simple for you; I'll give you the means and the motive to change." [Laughs.] And, so, then, I did get married. She and I headed off to Tokyo, my daughter was born there, and another life began. And so sometimes in your life, it's not so much about doing the right thing but recognizing it.

GK: This leads directly to the big issue in your films that no one has really spoken about, though it's right there in the prologues of the scripts to *American Gigolo* and *Light Sleeper:* the issue of love. In terms of the way it is presented in these two films and what you have just said, love is something that comes to us with a choice we have to make. While love has been central to your films, it has also really changed. Early on, it was a kind of big romantic Beatrice-type scenario . . .

PS: Yeah, it was an adjunct of the superego. It was another mountain to climb, another trophy to win. It was much more aggressive, whereas the secret of it is, in fact, quite passive. It's a lot harder to accept something than it is to take it. It's relatively easy to take something. We're all trained, especially men, to take things, and we're not so well trained to accept things.

GK: It definitely seems as if your later characters are learning how to accept love and its potential to transform things. This is what's happening at the end of *The Walker.* While Page has not exactly reinvented himself, he does seem to have found a way not to fossilize or curdle as Bob Crane does.

PS: And he's been hiding, hiding for a long time. Hiding under this sort of notion of being a black sheep, being the . . . the empty chair. Do you know what I mean by "the empty chair?"

GK: No, I don't.

PS: If you're having a dinner party and someone can't make it, the empty chair is the sort of man you call at the last minute, and he's very entertaining, something like that.

GK: I'd like to ask about the way the later characters are figured in terms of the issue of passivity. On one level, this term defines them well enough. But, on another level, it really doesn't do justice to the kinds of emotions with which these characters are struggling or their sense of melancholy and introspection. It's almost as if "passivity," especially in an American context, is a bad word. It's something an actor or spectator doesn't want to find in a character: "He or she was too passive. . . ." Whereas, in your films you have taken that negative stance and turned it into a chance to really explore all these other dimensions.

PS: It's interesting that when I came to *Dominion*, Liam Neeson was going to do it. And I had lunch with Liam, and he was trying to get out of it, and he eventually did. And the thing that was bothering him was that the character was too passive. And I was thinking, "What's wrong with that? Passive characters are really interesting too." But Liam wanted Merrin to be more in charge, and I was sort of surprised by that because that's not something I really think of in terms of an interesting character.

GK: Did Nolte have problems with that aspect of the script of *Affliction*?

PS: No, I don't know, you'd have to ask him. You know, it took him a long time to come around. But I think one of the reasons was money. I mean, that was the stated reason. It took him a long time to accept the fact that he wasn't going to get paid what he was getting at that time. But he gave an interview afterward, and he said, "If I had known this was going to be one of my most important roles, I would have done it a lot sooner." So, I'm not quite sure, it could very well have been.

GK: What he does with that character is extraordinary.

PS: What I really like about actors like Nick, like Stellan, is you can actually see their minds working. It's like they have a transparent forehead that you see those rusty wheels cranking around in their heads, you see them trying to put something together. [Laughs.]

GK: I wanted to ask you about your work with actors, because in *Affliction* you managed to coax such an extraordinary performance out of

Nolte. The performance of Dafoe in *Light Sleeper* is also a fascinating variation of the passive protagonist. When you're working on a script, do you give your actors a fair bit of room to interpret the role?

PS: Tony Perkins once said that he thought acting was 75 percent casting. I think it's about 90 percent casting. You get the right actor at the right time of his life, the right theme—all you have to do is modulate. Nick walked into rehearsals fully prepared—not only for his character. He had prepared the other characters in his head, too. And in rehearsals, I started changing how I was thinking about directing the film and how I was going to direct him. I said, "This guy is so in the zone on this character that I have to be careful not to fuck it up: don't get on him too much. The most interesting thing I'm seeing right now in rehearsals is watching Nick, and that's what I should do with the camera. Let's just watch this performance. Let's forget about all those tricks that you were thinking about. Just watch this performance." So . . . if you're lucky enough to have the right actor, right role, right time, then you're home. Providing, of course, the role is an interesting role.

GK: A few years ago you said, "I don't have the passion for filmmaking the way Marty does. I have a deep passion for telling stories and addressing moral issues. If the filmmaking tools were taken from me today, I would find other tools."[4] I was wondering what these other tools could be.

PS: Well, I've always had respect for Elia Kazan for being able to step away from directing and write books. I mean, they weren't great novels, but he was alive, and he was still creating. For me, I don't know what it would be. It would probably be some form of writing or study.

GK: What about the theater?

PS: Oh well, yeah. . . . Although, I don't know. I don't know if my sensibility's young enough for the theater that's happening right now. But who knows?

GK: Strange how things work.

PS: Yeah.

Notes

1. See Andrew's introduction to the first section of *The Image in Dispute* (5).

2. Soon after the interview, Schrader confirmed that Woody Harrelson had been signed to play the role of Carter Page.

3. Schrader qtd. in Powers (30).

4. Emery, *The Directors*.

Feature Films

Blue Collar (1978)
United States
Production: TAT Communications for Universal Pictures
Producers: Robin French, Don Guest, David Nicols
Distribution: Universal Pictures
Director: Paul Schrader
Screenplay: Paul Schrader, Leonard Schrader, based on material by Sydney
   A. Glass
Cinematography: Bobby Byrne
Editor: Tom Rolf
Production Design: Lawrence G. Paull
Costumes: Ron Dawson, Alice Rush
Music: Jack Nitzsche, Ry Cooder
Cast: Richard Pryor (Zeke Brown), Harvey Keitel (Jerry Bartowski), Yaphet
   Kotto (Smokey), Ed Begley Jr. (Bobby Joe), Harry Bellaver (Eddie
   Johnson), George Memmoli (Jenkins), Lucy Saroyan (Arlene Bartowski),
   Lane Smith (Clarence Hill), Cliff De Young (John Burrows), Borah Silver
   (Dogshit Miller), Chip Fields (Caroline Brown), Harry Northup (Hank)
Color
114 min.

Hardcore (1978)
United States
Production: A-Team for Columbia Pictures
Producers: John Milius, Buzz Feitshans
Distribution: Columbia Pictures
Director: Paul Schrader
Screenplay: Paul Schrader
Cinematography: Michael Chapman
Editing: Tom Rolf

Production Design: Paul Sylbert
Wardrobe Supervisors: Alice Rush, Tony Scarano
Music: Jack Nitzsche
Cast: George C. Scott (Jake VanDorn), Peter Boyle (Andy Mast), Season
   Hubley (Niki), Dick Sargent (Wes DeJong), Leonard Gaines (Ramada),
   David Nichols (Kurt), Gary Rand Graham (Tod), Larry Block (Detective
   Burrows), Marc Alaimo (Ratan), Leslie Ackerman (Felice), Charlotte
   McGinnes (Beatrice), Ilah Davis (Kristen VanDorn), Paul Martin (Joe
   VanDorn)
Color
108 min.

American Gigolo (1980)
United States
Production: Pierre Associates for Paramount Pictures
Producers: Freddie Fields, Jerry Bruckheimer
Distribution: Paramount Pictures
Director: Paul Schrader
Screenplay: Paul Schrader
Cinematography: John Bailey
Editing: Richard Halsey
Art director: Ed Richardson
Visual Consultant: Ferdinando Scarfiotti
Costumes: Giorgio Armani
Music: Giorgio Moroder
Cast: Richard Gere (Julian Kay), Lauren Hutton (Michelle Stratton), Hector
   Elizondo (Detective Sunday), Nina Van Pallandt (Anne), Bill Duke (Leon
   Jaimes), Brian Davies (Charles Stratton), K. Callan (Lisa Williams),
   Tom Stewart (Mr. Rheiman), Patti Carr (Judy Rheiman), David Cryer
   (Lieutenant Curtis), Carole Cook (Mrs. Dobrun), Carol Bruce (Mrs.
   Sloan), Frances Bergen (Mrs. Laudner)
Color
117 min.

Cat People (1982)
United States
Production: RKO Pictures/Universal Pictures
Producers: Jerry Bruckheimer, Charles Fries
Distribution: MCA/Universal Pictures
Director: Paul Schrader
Screenplay: Alan Ormsby, based on the script for *Cat People* (1943) by
   DeWitt Bodeen

Cinematography: John Bailey
Editing: Jacqueline Cambas, Bud Smith
Art Director: Edward Richardson
Visual Consultant: Ferdinando Scarfiotti
Costumes: Daniel Paredes
Music: Giorgio Moroder
Cast: Nastassia Kinski (Irena Gallier), Malcolm McDowell (Paul Gallier),
    John Heard (Oliver Yates), Annette O'Toole (Alice Perrin), Ruby Dee
    (Female), Ed Begley Jr. (Joe Creigh), Scott Paulin (Bill Searle), Frankie
    Faison (Detective Brandt), Ron Diamond (Detective Ron Diamond),
    Lynn Lowry (Ruthie), John Larroquette (Bronte Judson), Tessa Richarde
    (Billie), Patricia Perkins (Taxi driver), Berry Berenson (Sandra), Fausto
    Barajas (Otis)
Color
118 min.

Mishima: A Life in Four Chapters (1985)
United States
Production: Zoetrope Studios/Filmlink International/Lucasfilm Inc.
Producers: George Lucas, Francis Coppola, Mata Yamamoto, Tom Luddy
Distribution: Warner Brothers Pictures
Director: Paul Schrader
Screenplay: Paul Schrader, Leonard Schrader, Chieko Schrader, based on the
    novels *Temple of the Golden Pavilion, Kyoko's House,* and *Runaway Horses*
    by Yukio Mishima
Cinematography: John Bailey
Editing: Michael Chandler, Tomoyo Oshima
Production Design: Eiko Ishioka, Kazuo Takenaka
Costumes: Etsuko Yagyu
Music: Philip Glass
Narrator: Roy Scheider
Cast: *November 25, 1970:* Ken Ogata (Yukio Mishima), Masayuki Shionoya
    (Morita), Junkichi Orimoto (General Mashita);
Flashbacks: Naoko Otani (Mother), Go Riju (Mishima, age 18–19), Masato
    Aizawa (Mishima, age 9–14), Yuki Nagahara (Mishima, age 5), Haruko
    Kato (Grandmother);
Temple of the Golden Pavilion: Yasosuke Bando (Mizoguchi), Hisako Manda
    (Mariko), Naomi Oki (Girl), Miki Takakura (Girl), Imari Tsuji (Madame),
    Koichi Sato (Kashiwagi);
Kyoko's House: Kenji Sawada (Osamu), Reisen Lee (Kiyomi), Sachiko Hidari
    (Ozamu's mother), Setsuko Karasuma (Mitsuko), Tadanori Yokoo (Natsuo),
    Yasuaki Kurata (Takei);

Runaway Horses: Toshiyuki Nagashima (Isao), Hiroshi Katsuno (Lieutenant Hori), Naoya Makoto (Kendo instructor), Hiroki Ida (Izutsu), Jun Negami (Kurahara)
Color/Black and white
120 min.

Light of Day (1987)
United States
Production: Taft Entertainment Pictures/Keith Barish Productions/HBO
Producers: Doug Claybourne, Rob Cohen, Keith Barish, Alan Mark Poul
Distribution: TriStar Pictures
Director: Paul Schrader
Screenplay: Paul Schrader
Cinematography: John Bailey
Editing: Jacqueline Cambas
Production Design: Jeannine Claudia Oppewall
Costumes: Jodie Tillen
Music: Thomas Newman, Bruce Springsteen, and others
Cast: Michael J. Fox (Joe Rasnick), Gena Rowlands (Jeanette Rasnick), Joan Jett (Patti Rasnick), Michael McKean (Bu Montgomery), Thomas G. Waites (Smittie), Cherry Jones (Cindy Montgomery), Michael Dolan (Gene Bodine), Paul J. Harkins (Billy Tettore), Billy Sullivan (Benji Rasnick), Jason Miller (Benjamin Rasnick)
Color
107 min.

Patty Hearst (1988)
United Kingdom/United States
Production: Atlantic Entertainment Group/Zenith
Producers: Thomas Coleman, Michael Rosenblatt, Marvin Worth, Linda Reisman
Distribution: Atlantic Releasing Corporation
Director: Paul Schrader
Screenplay: Nicholas Kazan, based on the book *Every Secret Thing* by Patricia Campbell Hearst with Alvin Moscow
Cinematography: Bojan Bazelli
Editing: Michael R. Miller
Production Design: Jane Musky
Costumes: Richard Hornung
Music: Scott Johnson
Cast: Natasha Richardson (Patricia Hearst), William Forsythe (Teko), Ving Rhames (Cinque), Frances Fisher (Yolanda), Jodi Long (Wendy Yoshimura), Olivia Barash (Fahizah), Dana Delany (Gelina), Marek

Johnson (Zoya), Kitty Swink (Gabi), Peter Kowanko (Cujo), Tom O'Rourke (Jim Browning), Scott Kraft (Steven Weed), Jeff Imada (Neighbor), Ermal Williamson (Randolph A. Hearst), Elaine Revard (Catherine Hearst)
Color
108 min.

The Comfort of Strangers (1990)
Italy/United Kingdom
Production: Erre Produzioni/Sovereign Pictures/Reteitalia
Producers: Angelo Rizzoli, Mario Cotone, Linda Reisman, John Thompson
Distribution: Skouras Pictures
Director: Paul Schrader
Screenplay: Harold Pinter, based on the novel by Ian McEwan
Cinematography: Dante Spinotti
Editing: Bill Pankow
Production Design: Gianni Quaranta
Costumes: Giorgio Armani, Mariolina Bono
Music: Angelo Badalamenti
Cast: Christopher Walken (Robert), Rupert Everett (Colin), Natasha Richardson (Mary), Helen Mirren (Caroline), Manfredi Aliquo (Concierge), David Ford (Waiter), Daniel Franco (Waiter), Rossana Canghiari (Hotel maid), Fabrizio Castellani (Bar manager), Giancarlo Previati (First policeman), Antonio Serrano (Second policeman), Mario Cotone (Detective)
Color
107 min.

Light Sleeper (1992)
United States
Production: Grain of Sand Productions
Producer: Linda Reisman
Distribution: Fine Line Features
Director: Paul Schrader
Screenplay: Paul Schrader
Cinematography: Ed Lachman
Editing: Kristina Boden
Production Design: Richard Hornung
Costumes: Giorgio Armani
Music: Michael Been
Cast: Willem Dafoe (John LeTour), Susan Sarandon (Ann), Dana Delany (Marianne), David Clennon (Robert), Mary Beth Hurt (Teresa), Victor Garber (Tis), Jane Adams (Randi), Paul Jabara (Eddie), Robert Cicchini

(Guidone), Sam Rockwell (Jealous), Rene Rivera (Manuel), David Spade
(Theological cokehead)
Color
103 min.

Witch Hunt (1994)
United States
Production: Home Box Office/Pacific Western
Producers: Gale Ann Hurd, Michael R. Joyce
Director: Paul Schrader
Screenplay: Joseph Dougherty
Cinematography: Jean Yves Escoffier
Editing: Kristina Boden
Production Design: Curtis A. Schnell
Costumes: Jodie Tillen
Music: Angelo Badalamenti
Cast: Dennis Hopper (H. Philip Lovecraft), Penelope Ann Miller (Kim
    Hudson), Eric Bogosian (Senator Larson Crockett), Sherly Lee Ralph
    (Hypolyta Kropotkin), Julian Sands (Finn Macha), Alan Rosenberg (N. J.
    Gottlieb), Valerie Mahaffey (Trudy), John Epperson/Lypsinka (Vivian
    Dart), Debi Mazar (Manicurist), Gregory Bell (Shakespeare)
Color
100 min.

Touch (1997)
United States
Production: Initial Productions/Lumière International
Producers: Lila Cazes, Fida Attieh
Distribution: United Artists
Director: Paul Schrader
Screenplay: Paul Schrader, based on the novel by Elmore Leonard
Cinematography: Ed Lachman
Editing: Cara Silverman
Production Design: David Wasco
Costumes: Julie Weiss
Music: David Grohl
Cast: Skeet Ulrich (Juvenal), Bridget Fonda (Lynn Faulkner), Christopher
    Walken (Bill Hill), Tom Arnold (August Murray), Paul Mazursky (Artie),
    Gina Gershon (Debra Lusanne), Janeane Garofolo (Kathy Worthington),
    Lolita Davidovich (Antoinette Baker), Anthony Zerbe (Father Donahue),
    Richard Schiff (Jerry), L.L. Cool J (Himself)
Color
96 min.

Affliction (1997)
United States
Production: Kingsgate Productions/Largo Entertainment/JVC Entertainment
Producer: Linda Reisman
Distribution: Lions Gate Films Inc.
Director: Paul Schrader
Screenplay: Paul Schrader, based on the novel by Russell Banks
Cinematography: Paul Sarossy
Editing: Jay Rabinowitz
Production Design: Anne Pritchard
Costumes: François Laplante
Music: Michael Brook
Cast: Nick Nolte (Wade Whitehouse), Sissy Spacek (Margie Fogg), James
    Coburn (Glen Whitehouse), Willem Dafoe (Rolfe Whitehouse), Mary Beth
    Hurt (Lillian), Jim True (Jack Hewitt), Marian Seldes (Alma Pittman),
    Holmes Osborne (Gordon LaRiviere), Brigid Tierney (Jill), Sean McCann
    (Evan Twombley), Wayne Robson (Nick Wickham), Eugene Lipinski (J.
    Battle Hand)
Color
114 min.

Forever Mine (1999)
United Kingdom/Canada/United States
Production: J&M Entertainment/Moonstar Entertainment
Producers: Damita Nikapota, Kathleen Haase, Amy J. Kaufman
Distribution: J&M Entertainment
Director: Paul Schrader
Screenplay: Paul Schrader
Cinematography: John Bailey
Editing: Kristina Boden
Production Design: François Séguin
Costumes: Marit Allen
Music: Angelo Badalamenti
Cast: Joseph Fiennes (Manuel Esquema/Alan Riply), Ray Liotta (Mark
    Brice), Gretchen Mol (Ella Brice), Vincent Laresca (Javier Cesti), Myk
    Watford (Rick Martino), Lindsey Connell (Stewardess), Sean C. W.
    Johnson (Randy), Shawn Proctor (Cabana boy)
Color
115 min.

Auto Focus (2002)
United States
Production: Propaganda Films/Good Machine/Focus Puller Inc.
Producers: Scott Alexander, Larry Karaszewski, Todd Rosken, Pat Dollard,
  Alicia Allain
Distribution: Sony Pictures Classics
Director: Paul Schrader
Screenplay: Michael Gerbosi, based on the book *The Murder of Bob Crane*
  by Robert Graysmith
Cinematography: Fred Murphy
Editing: Kristina Boden
Production Design: James Chinlund
Costumes: Julie Weiss
Music: Angelo Badalamenti
Cast: Greg Kinnear (Bob Crane), Willem Dafoe (John Carpenter), Rita
  Wilson (Ann Crane), Maria Bello (Patricia Olsen/Patricia Crane), Ron
  Leibman (Lenny), Bruce Solomon (Edward H. Feldman), Michael
  Rodgers (Richard Dawson), Kurt Fuller (Werner Klemperer), Christopher
  Neiman (Robert Clay), Lyle Kanouse (John Banner), Donnamarie Recco
  (Melissa/Mistress Victoria), Ed Begley Jr. (Mel Rosen)
Color
105 min.

Dominion: Prequel to the Exorcist (2005)
United States
Production: Morgan Creek Productions
Producer: James G. Robinson
Distribution: Warner Brothers Pictures
Director: Paul Schrader
Screenplay: William Wisher, Caleb Carr
Cinematography: Vittorio Storaro
Editing: Tim Silano
Production Design: John Graysmark
Costumes: Luke Reichle
Music: Trevor Rabin, Angelo Badalamenti, Dog Fashion Disco
Cast: Stellan Skarsgård (Father Lankester Merrin), Gabriel Mann (Father
  Francis), Clara Bellar (Rachel Lesno), Billy Crawford (Cheche), Ralph
  Brown (Sergeant Major), Antoine Kamerling (Kessel), Israel Aduramo
  (Jomo), Julian Wadham (Major Granville), Andrew French (Chuma)
Color
117 min.

The Walker (2007)
United States/United Kingdom
Production: Kintop Pictures, Ingenious Film Partners and Asia Pacific Films in association with Isle of Man Film
Producer: Deepak Nayar
Director: Paul Schrader
Screenplay: Paul Schrader
Cinematography: Chris Seager BSC
Editing: Julian Rodd
Production Design: James Merifield
Costumes: Nic Ede
Cast: Woody Harrelson (Carter Page III), Kristin Scott Thomas (Lynn Lockner), Lauren Bacall (Natalie Van Miter), Ned Beatty (Jack Delorean), Moritz Bleibtreu (Emek Yoglu), Mary Beth Hurt (Chrissie Morgan), Lily Tomlin (Abigail Delorean), Willem Dafoe (Senator Larry Lockner), William Hope (Mungo Tenant), Geff Francis (Detective Dixon), Steven Hartley (Robbie Kononsberg), Garrick Hagon (John Krebs), Michael J. Reynolds (Ethan Withal), Allen Lidkey (Andrew, salesperson), Stewart Alexander (Edgar), Andres Williams (Radley), Jason Durran (police officer), Marcello Cabezas (photographer)
Color
108 min.

Short Films

Tight Connection (1985)
United States
Producer: Alan Poul
Director: Paul Schrader
Screenplay: Paul Schrader
Cinematography: Makoto Hishida
Cast: Bob Dylan, Mitsuko Baisho, Mary Jane Adams
Color
6 min.

New Blue (1995)
United Kingdom
Production: Arts Council/BBC
Producer: Mitch Gross
Director: Paul Schrader
Cinematography: Mitch Gross
Editing: Adrienne Berofsky
Color
5 min.

Screenplays

The Yakuza (1975)
United States/Japan
Production: Warner Brothers/Toei Co. Ltd.
Producers: Shundo Koji, Sydney Pollack, Michael Hamilburg
Distribution: Warner Brothers
Director: Sydney Pollack
Screenplay: Paul Schrader, Leonard Schrader, Robert Towne
Cinematography: Okazaki Kozo, Duke Callaghan
Editing: Fredric Steinkamp, Thomas Standford, Don Guidice
Production Design: Stephen Grimes
Costumes: Dorothy Jeakins
Music: Dave Grusin
Cast: Robert Mitchum (Harry Kilmer), Takakura Ken (Tanaka Ken), Brian
    Keith (George Tanner), Kishi Keiko (Tanaka Eiko), Okada Eiji (Tono
    Toshiro), James Shigeta (Goro), Herb Edelman (Oliver Wheat)
Color
112 min.

Taxi Driver (1976)
United States
Production: Bill/Phillips and Columbia Pictures
Producers: Michael Phillips, Julia Phillips
Distribution: Columbia Pictures
Director: Martin Scorsese
Screenplay: Paul Schrader
Cinematography: Michael Chapman
Editing: Marcia Lucas, Tom Rolf, Melvin Shapiro
Art Director: Charles Rosen
Visual Consultant: David Nicols
Costumes: Ruth Morley
Music: Bernard Herrmann
Cast: Robert De Niro (Travis Bickle), Jodie Foster (Iris), Cybill Shepherd
    (Betsy), Harvey Keitel (Sport), Albert Brooks (Tom), Peter Boyle (Wizard),
    Leonard Harris (Charles Palantine), Steven Prince (Andy, the gun
    salesman), Diahnne Abbott (Concession girl), Frank Adu (Angry black
    man), Martin Scorsese (Passenger watching silhouette)
Color
113 min.

Obsession (1976)
United States
Production: Yellow Bird Films
Producers: Robert S. Bremson, George Litto, Harry N. Blum
Distribution: Columbia Pictures
Director: Brian De Palma
Screenplay: Paul Schrader, Brian De Palma
Cinematography: Vilmos Zsigmond
Editing: Paul Hirsch
Art Director: Jack Senter
Visual Consultant: Anne Pritchard
Costumes: Frank Balchus
Music: Bernard Herrmann
Cast: Cliff Robertson (Michael Courtland), Genevieve Bujold (Elizabeth
    Courtland/Sandra Pontinari), John Lithgow (Robert LaSalle), Sylvia
    "Kuumba" Williams (Judy), Wanda Blackman (Amy Courtland), Patrick
    McNamara (Third kidnapper), Stanley J. Reyes (Inspector Brie)
Color
98 min.

Rolling Thunder (1977)
United States
Production: American International Pictures
Producers: Lawrence Gordon, Norman T. Herman
Distribution: American International Pictures
Director: John Flynn
Screenplay: Paul Schrader, Heywood Gould
Cinematography: Jordan Cronenweth
Editing: Frank P. Keller
Art Director: Steve Berger
Music: Barry De Vorzon
Cast: William Devane (Major Charles Rane), Tommy Lee Jones (Johnny
    Vohden), Linda Haynes (Linda Forchet), Lisa Richards (Janet), Dabney
    Coleman (Maxwell), James Best (Texan), Cassie Yates (Candy), Luke
    Askew (Automatic Slim), Lawrason Driscoll (Cliff), Jordan Gerler (Mark),
    James Victor (Lopez)
Color
99 min.

Old Boyfriends (1979)
United States
Production: Edward R. Pressman Productions
Producers: Paul Schrader, Edward R. Pressman, Michele Rappaport

Distribution: AVCO Embassy Pictures
Director: Joan Tewkesbury
Screenplay: Paul Schrader, Leonard Schrader
Cinematography: William A. Fraker
Editing: Marcia Lucas, Tom Rolf, Melvin Shapiro
Costumes: Tony Fasco, Suzanne Grace
Music: David Shire
Cast: Talia Shire (Dianne Cruise), Richard Jordan (Jeff Turin), John Belushi
    (Eric Katz), Keith Carradine (Wayne Vantil), John Houseman (Dr.
    Hoffman), Buck Henry (Art Kopple), Bethel Leslie (Mrs. Vantil), Joan
    Hotchkis (Pamela Shaw)
Color
103 min.

Raging Bull (1980)
United States
Production: Chartoff-Winkler Productions/United Artists
Producers: Irwin Winkler, Robert Chartoff, Peter Savage
Distribution: United Artists
Director: Martin Scorsese
Screenplay: Paul Schrader, Mardik Martin, based on the book *Raging Bull* by
    Jake La Motta with Joseph Carter, Peter Savage
Cinematography: Michael Chapman
Editing: Thelma Schoonmaker
Production Design: Gene Rudolf
Costumes: Richard Bruno
Cast: Robert De Niro (Jake La Motta), Cathy Moriarty (Vickie La Motta), Joe
    Pesci (Joey La Motta), Frank Vincent (Salvy), Nicholas Colasanto (Tommy
    Como), Theresa Saldana (Lenore), Mario Gallo (Mario), Frank Adonis
    (Patsy), Joseph Bono (Guido), Frank Topham (Toppy), Lori Anne Flax
    (Irma), Charles Scorsese (Charlie), Don Dunphy (Himself), Mardik Martin
    (Copa waiter), Martin Scorsese (Barbizon stagehand)
Black and white/Color
129 min.

The Mosquito Coast (1986)
United States
Production: The Saul Zaentz Company/Jerome Hellman Productions/Warner
    Brothers
Producers: Saul Zaentz, Jerome Hellman
Distribution: Warner Brothers
Director: Peter Weir
Screenplay: Paul Schrader, based on the novel by Paul Theroux

Cinematography: John Seale
Editing: Thom Noble, Richard Francis-Bruce
Production Design: John Stoddart
Costumes: Gary Jones
Music: Maurice Jarre
Cast: Harrison Ford (Allie Fox), Helen Mirren (Mother), River Phoenix
   (Charlie Fox), Jadrien Steele (Jerry Fox), Hilary Gordon (April Fox),
   Rebecca Gordon (Clover Fox), Jason Alexander (Clerk), Dick O'Neill (Mr.
   Polski), André Gregory (Reverend Spellgood)
Color
119 min.

The Last Temptation of Christ (1988)
United States
Production: Universal Pictures/Cineplex Odeon Films
Producer: Barbara De Fina
Distribution: Universal Pictures
Director: Martin Scorsese
Screenplay: Paul Schrader, based on the novel by Nikos Kazantzakis
Cinematography: Michael Ballhaus
Editing: Thelma Schoonmaker
Production Design: John Beard
Costumes: Jean-Pierre Delifer
Music: Peter Gabriel
Cast: Willem Dafoe (Jesus), Harvey Keitel (Judas), Paul Greco (Zealot),
   Steven Shill (Centurion), Verna Bloom (Mary, Mother of Jesus), Barbara
   Hershey (Mary Magdalene), Roberts Blossom (Aged Master), Barry Miller
   (Jeroboam), Gary Basaraba (Andrew Apostle), Irvin Kershner (Zebedee),
   Victor Argo (Peter Apostle), Michael Been (John Apostle), Paul Herman
   (Phillip Apostle), John Lurie (James Apostle), Leo Burmester (Nathaniel
   Apostle), Andre Gregory (John the Baptist), Harry Dean Stanton (Saul/
   Paul), David Bowie (Pontius Pilate)
Color
163 min.

City Hall (1996)
United States
Production: Castle Rock Entertainment/Columbia Pictures Corporation
Producers: Edward R. Pressman, Charles Mulvehill, Harold Becker, Ken
   Lipper
Distribution: Columbia Pictures
Director: Harold Becker
Screenplay: Ken Lipper, Paul Schrader, Nicholas Pileggi, Bo Goldman

Cinematography: Michael Seresin, Jamie Silverstein
Editing: David Bretherton, Robert C. Jones
Production Design: Jane Musky
Costumes: Richard Hornung
Music: Jerry Goldsmith
Cast: Al Pacino (Mayor John Pappas), John Cusack (Deputy Mayor Kevin
    Calhoun), Bridget Fonda (Marybeth Cogan), Danny Aiello (Frank
    Anselmo), Martin Landau (Judge Walter Stern), David Paymer (Abe
    Goodman), Tony Franciosa (Paul Zapatti), Richard Schiff (Larry Schwartz),
    Lindsay Duncan (Sydney Pappas), Nestor Serrano (Detective Eddie
    Santos), Mel Winkler (Detective Albert Holly)
Color
111 min.

Bringing Out the Dead (1999)
United States
Production: De Fina-Cappa/Paramount Pictures/Touchstone Pictures
Producers: Scott Rudin, Barbara De Fina
Distribution: Paramount Pictures
Director: Martin Scorsese
Screenplay: Paul Schrader, based on the novel by Joe Connelly
Cinematography: Robert Richardson
Editing: Thelma Schoonmaker
Production Design: Dante Ferretti
Costumes: Rita Ryack
Music: Elmer Bernstein
Cast: Nicolas Cage (Frank Pierce), Patricia Arquette (Mary Burke), John
    Goodman (Larry), Ving Rhames (Marcus), Tom Sizemore (Tom Wolls),
    Marc Anthony (Noel), Mary Beth Hurt (Nurse Constance), Cliff Curtis
    (Cy Coates), Nestor Serrano (Dr. Hazmat), Aida Turturro (Nurse Crupp),
    Sonja Sohn (Kanita), Cynthia Roman (Rose), Afemo Omilami (Griss),
    Cullen Oliver Johnson (Mr. Burke), Arthur Nascarella (Captain Barney),
    Martin Scorsese (Dispatcher)
Color
121 min.

Alighieri, Dante. *Vita Nuova*. Trans. Mark Musa. Oxford: Oxford University Press, 1992.

Andrew, Dudley. *The Image in Dispute: Art and Cinema in the Age of Photography*. Austin: University of Texas Press, 1997.

Banner, Simon. "From Bed to Worse." *Time Out*, November 28, 1990, 18–20.

Bazin, André. "The Ontology of the Photographic Image." In *What Is Cinema?* Ed. and trans. Hugh Gray. Berkeley: University of California Press, 1967. 9–16.

Benjamin, Walter. "The Storyteller: Reflections on the Works of Nikolai Leskov." In *Illuminations*. Ed. Hannah Arendt. Trans. Harry Zohn. Suffolk: Fontana/Collins, 1979. 83–109.

Blanchot, Maurice. *The Space of Literature*. Trans. Ann Smock. Lincoln: University of Nebraska Press, 1982.

Bliss, Michael. "Affliction and Forgiveness: An Interview with Paul Schrader." *Film Quarterly* 54.1 (Fall 2000): 2–9.

Bouzereau, Laurent, dir. *Making Taxi Driver*. On *Taxi Driver* DVD. Columbia Pictures, 1999.

Bragg, Melvyn, host. *The South Bank Show: Schrader*. London: London Weekend Television, 1989.

Carroll, Noël. "The Future of Allusion: Hollywood in the Seventies (and Beyond)." *October* 20 (Spring 1982): 51–81.

Caruth, Cathy. "Trauma and Experience." Introduction to *Trauma: Explorations in Memory*. Ed. Cathy Caruth. Baltimore: Johns Hopkins University Press, 1995. 3–12.

Combs, Richard. "Patty Hearst and Paul Schrader: A Life and a Career in 14 Stations." *Sight and Sound* 58.3 (Summer 1989): 196–201.

————. Review of *Cortesie per gli ospiti* (*The Comfort of Strangers*). *Monthly Film Bulletin* 58.684 (January 1991): 5–6.

————. Review of *American Gigolo*. *Monthly Film Bulletin* 47.556 (May 1980): 87–88.

————. Review of *Mishima: A Life in Four Chapters*. *Monthly Film Bulletin* 52.621 (October 1985): 299–301.

Comolli, Jean-Louis. "Historical Fiction: A Body Too Much." *Screen* 19.2 (1978): 41–53.

Cook, Bruce. "Talents." *American Film* 5.3 (December 1979): 29, 58–62.

Cook, David A. *Lost Illusions: American Cinema in the Shadow of Watergate and Vietnam, 1970–1979.* Vol. 9 of *History of the American Cinema.* Berkeley: University of California Press, 2000.

Cousins, Mark, dir. *Scene by Scene with Paul Schrader.* BBC Scotland, 1998.

Crowdus, Gary, and Dan Georgakas. "*Blue Collar:* An Interview with Paul Schrader." *Cineaste* 8.3 (1978): 34–37, 59.

Custen, George F. *Bio/Pics: How Hollywood Constructed Public History.* New Brunswick, N.J.: Rutgers University Press, 1992.

Deleuze, Gilles. *Cinema 1: The Movement-Image.* Trans. Hugh Tomlinson and Barbara Habberjam. Minneapolis: University of Minnesota Press, 1986.

———. *Cinema 2: The Time-Image.* Trans. Hugh Tomlinson and Robert Galeta. Minneapolis: University of Minnesota Press, 1989.

Diderot, Denis. *The Paradox of Acting.* Trans. Walter Herries Pollock. With *Masks or Faces?* by William Archer. Intro. Lee Strasberg. New York: Hill and Wang, 1957.

Dunne, John Gregory. "The Conversation: John Gregory Dunne and Paul Schrader." *Esquire* 98 (July 1982): 85–93.

Elsaesser, Thomas. "American Auteur Cinema: The Last—or First—Great Picture Show." In *The Last Great American Picture Show: New Hollywood Cinema in the 1970s.* Ed. Thomas Elsaesser, Alexander Horwath, and Noel King. Amsterdam: Amsterdam University Press, 2004. 37–69.

———. "The Pathos of Failure: American Films in the 1970s; Notes on the Unmotivated Hero." In *The Last Great American Picture Show: New Hollywood Cinema in the 1970s.* Ed. Thomas Elsaesser, Alexander Horwath, and Noel King. Amsterdam: Amsterdam University Press, 2004. 279–92.

Emery, Robert J., dir. *The Directors: The Films of Paul Schrader.* American Film Institute, 2001.

Epstein, Jean. "Ciné-Mystique." Trans. Stuart Liebman. *Millennium Film Journal* 10–11 (Fall–Winter 1981–82): 191–93.

Foucault, Michel. *Remarks on Marx: Conversations with Duccio Trombadori.* Trans. R. James Goldstein and James Cascaito. New York: Semiotext(e), 1991.

Fraser, Peter. "*American Gigolo* and Transcendental Style." *Literature Film Quarterly* 16.2 (1988): 91–100.

Fuchs, Cynthia. "'I Got Some Bad Ideas in My Head.'" In *Film Analysis: A Norton Reader.* New York: W. W. Norton and Co., 2005. 696–714.

Herdman, John. *The Double in Nineteenth-Century Fiction.* Basingstoke: Macmillan, 1990.

Hindes, Andrew, and Benedict Carver. "Distribs Roll Out the Un-welcome Mat." *Variety* 369 (February 9–15, 1998): 1, 87.

Isenberg, Nancy. "Not 'Anyone's Daughter': Patty Hearst and the Postmodern Legal Subject." *American Quarterly* 52.4 (2000): 639–81.

Jaehne, Karen. "Patty Who? Hearst on the Street." *Film Comment* 24.4 (July–August 1988): 24–26.

———. "Schrader's *Mishima:* An Interview." *Film Quarterly* 39.3 (Spring 1986): 11–17.

Jackson, Kevin. "Blood on the Tracks." *Sight and Sound* 1.6 (1991): 24–27.

———. Introduction to *Schrader on Schrader,* by Paul Schrader. Ed. Kevin Jackson. London: Faber and Faber, 1990. ix–xix.

Joyce, Cynthia. "On His Own Turf." *Salon Entertainment.* January 7, 1999. Accessed January 3, 2002. http://www.salon.com/ent/movies/int/1999/01/07int.html.

Kaplan, Michael. "Questions for Paul Schrader: The Art of Darkness." *New York Times Magazine,* October 24, 1999, 35.

Levy, Emanuel. *Cinema of Outsiders: The Rise of American Independent Film.* New York: New York University Press, 1999.

Liebman, Stuart. "Introduction to Jean Epstein's 'Ciné-Mystique.'" *Millennium Film Journal* 10–11 (Fall–Winter 1981–82): 186–90.

Martin, Adrian. "*Fingers.*" *Flesh* 21–22 (1988): 14–23.

———. "Fuck Him or Fight Him: Will and Representation in Martin Scorsese." *Scripsi* 8.1 (August 1992): 147–59.

———. *Once upon a Time in America.* London: BFI, 1998.

Mortimer, Lorraine. "Blood Brothers: Purity, Masculinity, and the Flight from the Feminine in Scorsese and Schrader." *Cinema Papers* 75 (September 1989): 30–36.

———. "Desperately Seeking Union: Paul Schrader and *Light Sleeper.*" *Metro* 94 (Winter 1993): 4–6.

Nichols, Bill. "*American Gigolo:* Transcendental Style and Narrative Form." *Film Quarterly* 34.4 (Summer 1981): 8–13.

Patterson, Patricia, and Manny Farber. "The Power and the Gory." *Film Comment* 12.3 (May–June 1976): 26–30.

Perez, Gilberto. "Antonioni and Vitti." Booklet. *Michelangelo Antonioni's L'Eclisse* DVD. Criterion Collection, 2005. 14–19.

Pinter, Harold. *Collected Screenplays Three.* London: Faber and Faber, 2000.

Polan, Dana. "Auteur Desire." *Screening the Past* 12 (2001). Accessed July 6, 2004. http://www.latrobe.edu.au/screeningthepast/firstrelease/fr0301/dpfr12a.htm.

Powers, John. "The True Believer." *L.A. Weekly,* October 18–24, 2002, 26–27, 29–30.

Prince, Stephen. *A New Pot of Gold: Hollywood under the Electronic Rainbow, 1980–1989.* Vol. 10 of *History of the American Cinema.* Berkeley: University of California Press, 2000.

Ray, Robert B. *A Certain Tendency of the Hollywood Cinema, 1930–1980.* Princeton, N.J.: Princeton University Press, 1985.

Rayns, Tony. "Truth with the Power of Fiction." *Sight and Sound* 53.4 (Autumn 1984): 256–60.

Rebello, Stephen. "*Cat People:* Paul Schrader Changes His Spots." *American Film* 7.6 (1982): 38–45.

Rechler, Glenn. "An Interview with Paul Schrader." *Cineaste* 17.1 (1989): 31.

Romney, Jonathan. "Following the Tour Guide." *Monthly Film Bulletin* 58.684 (January 1991): 6–7.

———. "New Ways to Skin a Cat: Paul Schrader's *Cat People.*" *Enclitic* 8.1–2 (Spring–Fall 1984): 148–55.

Rosenbaum, Jonathan. "New Hollywood and the Sixties Melting Pot." In *The Last Great American Picture Show: New Hollywood Cinema in the 1970s.* Ed. Thomas Elsaesser, Alexander Horwath, and Noel King. Amsterdam: Amsterdam University Press, 2004. 131–52.

Ruppert, Jeanne M., ed. *Gender: Literary and Cinematic Representation; Selected Papers from the Eleventh Annual Florida State University Conference on Literature and Film.* Gainsville: University Press of Florida, 1994.

Sarris, Andrew. "Old Movies, Old Times." *Village Voice,* April 13, 1982, 43.

Schrader, Paul. "Canon Fodder." *Film Comment* 42.5 (September–October 2006): 33–49.

———. *Collected Screenplays 1: Taxi Driver, American Gigolo, Light Sleeper.* London: Faber and Faber, 2002.

———. *Transcendental Style in Film: Ozu, Bresson, Dreyer.* Cambridge, Mass.: Da Capo Press, 1972.

———. *Schrader on Schrader, and Other Writings.* Revised ed. Ed. Kevin Jackson. London: Faber and Faber, 2004.

Sinyard, Neil. "Guilty Pleasures: The Films of Paul Schrader." *Cinema Papers* 41 (December 1982): 510–15.

Smith, Gavin. "Awakenings." *Film Comment* 28.2 (March–April 1992): 50–52, 54–59.

Stern, Lesley. *The Scorsese Connection.* London: BFI, 1995.

Taubin, Amy. *Taxi Driver.* London: BFI, 2000.

Taylor, Charles. "History Repeats Itself." *Salon Entertainment.* January 8, 1999. Accessed January 2002. http://www.salon.com/ent/movies/reviews/1999/01/08reviewb.html.

Thompson, Richard. "Screenwriter: *Taxi Driver's* Paul Schrader Interviewed by Richard Thompson." *Film Comment* 12.2 (March–April 1976): 6–19.

Thomson, David. "Cats." *Film Comment* 18.2 (March–April 1982): 49–52.

Webster, Duncan. "Nobody's Patsy: Versions of Patty Hearst." *Critical Quarterly* 32.1 (Spring 1990): 3–21.

Williams, Linda Ruth. "Swing High, Swing Low." *Sight and Sound* 13.3 (March 2003): 32–33, 36.

Willis, Sharon. "Seductive Spaces: Private Fascinations and Public Fantasies in Popular Cinema." In *Seduction and Theory: Readings of Gender, Representation, and Rhetoric.* Ed. Dianne Hunter. Urbana: University of Illinois Press, 1989. 47–70.

Wilson, John Howard. "Sources for a Neglected Masterpiece: Paul Schrader's *Mishima.*" *Biography* 20.3 (Summer 1997): 264–83.

Wood, Robin. *Hollywood from Vietnam to Reagan . . . and Beyond.* Expanded and revised ed. New York: Columbia University Press, 2003.

Books in the series
Contemporary Film Directors

George Kouvaros is associate professor in film in the
School of English, Media, and Performing Arts at the
University of New South Wales, Sydney. He is the author
of *Where Does It Happen? John Cassavetes and Cinema
at the Breaking Point* and coeditor, with Lesley Stern, of
Falling for You: Essays on Cinema and Performance.

The University of Illinois Press
is a founding member of the
Association of American University Presses.

Composed in 10/13 New Caledonia
with Helvetica Neue display
by Jim Proefrock
at the University of Illinois Press
Designed by Paula Newcomb
Manufactured by Sheridan Books, Inc.

University of Illinois Press
1325 South Oak Street
Champaign, IL 61820-6903
www.press.uillinois.edu